D0919644

# ‹FRANCE›

# MAJOR WORLD NATIONS

# FRANCE

Brian Sookram

## CHELSEA HOUSE PUBLISHERS
### Philadelphia

**Chelsea House Publishers**

*Contributing Author:* W. Douglass Paschall

First Printing

1   3   5   7   9   8   6   4   2

Library of Congress Cataloging-in-Publication Data applied for

ISBN 0–7910–4738–5

# ◄CONTENTS►

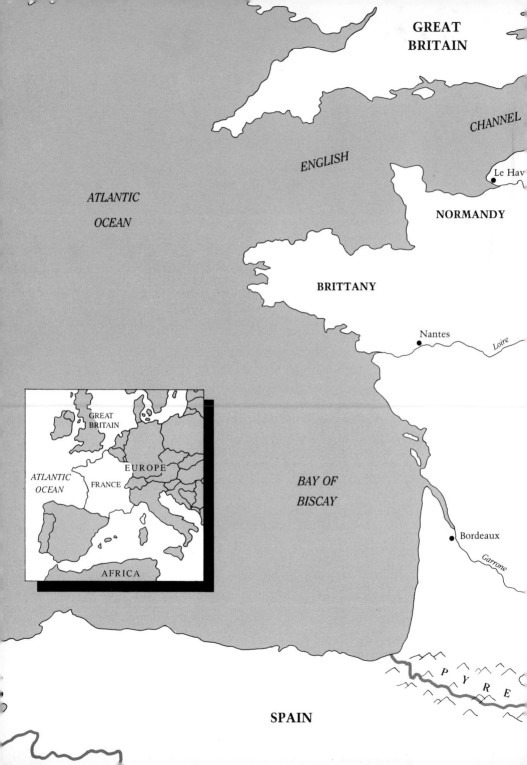

GREAT
BRITAIN

CHANNEL

ENGLISH

Le Hav

ATLANTIC

OCEAN

NORMANDY

BRITTANY

Nantes

Loire

GREAT
BRITAIN

ATLANTIC
OCEAN

EUROPE

FRANCE

BAY OF

BISCAY

Bordeaux

Garonne

AFRICA

P Y R E

SPAIN

NORTH SEA

Dunkerque

FLANDERS

Lille

BELGIUM

Rhine

River

LUXEMBOURG

GERMANY

ARDENNES

Oise River

Seine

Paris

Versailles

LORRAINE

VOSGES

ALSACE

Strasbourg

River

Orléans

River

J U R A

S

P

FRANCE

SWITZERLAND

L

A

Lyons

Mont
Blanc

ITALY

MASSIF
CENTRAL

Rhône River

MONACO

Cannes

Nice

Marseilles

RIVIERA

River

GULF OF LYONS

Corsica

N
E
E
S

ANDORRA

MEDITERRANEAN        SEA

# ◄ FACTS AT A GLANCE ►

## Land and People

| | |
|---|---|
| Area | 213,010 square miles (553,826 square kilometers) |
| Highest Point | Mont Blanc, 15,771 feet (4,807 meters) |
| Capital | Paris (population 2.2 million, city; 10.7 million, region) |
| Major Cities | Lyons (population 1.3 million), Marseilles (population 1.2 million), Lille (population 1 million) |
| Major Rivers | Garonne, Rhône, Seine, Loire, Rhine |
| Major Mountain Ranges | Alps, Pyrenees, Massif Central, Jura, Vosges |
| Population | 58 million |
| Population Density | 276 people per square mile (107 per square kilometer) |
| Population Distribution | Urban, 74 percent; rural, 26 percent |
| Language | French |
| Racial Groups | White, about 95 percent; nonwhite, about 5 percent |
| Literacy Rate | 99 percent |
| Religions | Roman Catholic, 81 percent; Muslim, 6.9 percent; Protestant, 1.7 percent; Jewish, 1.3 percent |

| Average Life Expectancy | Women, 82 years; men, 74 years |

## Economy

| Natural Resources | Iron ore, bauxite, coal, forests |
| Major Products | Automobiles, chemicals, textiles, steel, aircraft, agricultural products, wine |
| Chief Imports | Oil, machinery, agricultural products |
| Chief Exports | Manufactured goods, chemicals, wine, foodstuffs |
| Gross Domestic Product | Equal to U.S. $1.5 trillion |
| Employment of Work Force | Services, 69 percent; industry, 27 percent; agriculture, 4 percent |
| Currency | Franc (5.7 francs equaled U.S. $1 in 1997) |
| Average Net Annual Income | Equal to about U.S. $26,000 |

## Government

| Form of Government | Multiparty republic with a legislative branch consisting of a National Assembly and a Senate |
| Municipal Administration | Regions that contain departments (similar to U.S. states), divided into *arrondissements* (similar to U. S. counties), subdivided into *communes*, or townships. |
| Head of State | President, elected to a seven-year term |
| Head of Government | Prime minister, appointed by the president |
| Eligibility to Vote | French citizens of at least 18 years of age can vote in the presidential elections, in the governmental elections for the National Assembly, and in the municipal elections |

# ◄HISTORY AT A GLANCE►

| | |
|---|---|
| 600 B.C. | The Ligurians and the Gauls inhabit the area that is now France. |
| 52 B.C. | France, known as Gaul, is conquered by the Romans, led by Julius Caesar. Roman civilization spreads. |
| circa 500 | The German tribes of Franks, Visigoths, and Burgundians migrate to Gaul. The Franks, under Clovis, drive out the Romans and take the land for themselves. Clovis establishes the Merovingian dynasty. |
| 751 | Pippin the Short becomes the first king of the Carolingian dynasty. |
| 768–814 | Charlemagne increases the size of the empire, brings organized government to Gaul, and supports education, literature, and the arts. |
| 987 | Hugh Capet is proclaimed king and begins the 800-year reign of the Capetian dynasty. |
| 1337 | The Hundred Years' War between France and England begins. |
| 1429 | Joan of Arc leads the French army to save the city of Orléans from capture by the English. The French eventually drive the English from France in 1453, ending the war. |

about 1550   The Catholics wage the Wars of Religion against the Huguenots, or Protestants.

1610   Louis XIII ascends the French throne. France flourishes, due mainly to Louis's prime minister, Cardinal Richelieu, who directs the country's overseas expansion.

1643–1715   King Louis XIV, called the Sun King, reigns. He spends extravagantly and depletes the country's resources.

1774   Louis XVI becomes king.

July 14, 1789   A Parisian mob storms the Bastille, beginning the French Revolution.

Aug.–Oct. 1789   The National Assembly abolishes the ancien régime and adopts the Declaration of the Rights of Man and of the Citizen.

1792   The First Republic is proclaimed.

1793–94   Louis XVI is put on trial, found guilty, and executed. The Committee of Public Safety begins the Reign of Terror and orders numerous guillotine executions.

1799   Napoléon Bonaparte seizes power and installs himself as first consul. Five years later the people allow him to take the title of emperor.

1811   Napoléon achieves the conquest of most of western Europe.

1813–14   England, Prussia, Austria, and Russia form an alliance to depose Napoléon. Louis XVIII is proclaimed king of France.

1830   Discontented with the king's attempts to restore the ancien régime, the people revolt. King Charles X abdicates and is replaced by the Citizen King, Louis Philippe.

| | |
|---|---|
| 1848–49 | The people revolt again and Louis Phillippe flees Paris. A new constitution is written and the Second Republic is formed. Louis-Napoléon, nephew of Napoléon Bonaparte, is elected president. |
| 1852 | Louis-Napoléon is declared Emperor Napoléon III; the Second Empire begins. |
| 1870–71 | The Franco-Prussian War is fought. France is defeated and the Second Empire falls. |
| 1875 | With a new constitution, the Third Republic is founded. |
| 1914–18 | France enters World War I; the country is devastated. Almost 1.5 million Frenchmen die in battle. |
| 1940–44 | German Nazis occupy Paris during World War II. General Charles de Gaulle leads the Free French outside France. |
| 1946 | The Fourth Republic is formed. Great political instability accompanies economic recovery. |
| 1958 | De Gaulle draws up a new constitution and, as president, heads the Fifth Republic. His is re-elected in 1965. |
| 1969 | De Gaulle resigns. |
| 1974–1981 | President Valéry Giscard d'Estaing reforms many laws. |
| 1981–95 | Socialist government of François Mitterrand places much of the economy under government control, followed by a period of reprivatization. France enters the European Union. |
| 1995 | Conservative president Jacques Chirac is elected, vowing to fight unemployment. |

*Parisians throng the banks of the Seine River on the night of July 14—Bastille Day. Spectacular fireworks cap a day of celebration commemorating the beginning of the French Revolution.*

# France and the World

In the late 1700s, one of the most significant revolutions in the history of humankind took place. Every throne in Europe shook and every monarch in the world trembled during the 10 years of the French Revolution. Beginning with the fall of the Bastille on July 14, 1789, and ending with the rise to power of Napoléon Bonaparte in 1799, this tremendous social upheaval rocked the world. The changes that it set in motion are still having an impact more than two centuries later.

The Revolution was begun by France's peasants. After more than a century of bitter poverty, they rose up against rulers who had oppressed them, had taxed them heavily, had mismanaged the country's finances, and had impoverished the nation's industries. The French Declaration of the Rights of Man and of the Citizen, drafted in 1789, became one of the foundations of human rights and democratic governments throughout the world.

The concept of nationalism—that is, of pride in one's country and in its independence—had developed several centuries earlier in France, as illustrated by the inspiring story of Joan of Arc. At the age of 17, Joan led an army that defeated English forces at the city of Orléans in the 15th century. And like French nationalism, French culture developed before the Revolution and has had a wide influence. During the reign of Louis XIV, in the 17th century, France's literature and fine arts flourished—and made a strong impact throughout Europe. Today, French culture continues to be world renowned.

The creative imagination and the variety that characterize traditional French products in such fields as fashion, arts and crafts, and perfume make them among the most appealing on the world market. Additionally, France is the number one agricultural producer in Western Europe and ranks among the world's foremost producers and exporters of wine, milk, meat, and cereals.

The Republic of France is also a country of outstanding scientific and industrial achievements. The nation ranks first in the world in aircraft and aerospace industries and is the third greatest exporter in the metalworking industry and the fourth greatest exporter of chemicals.

France also faces the responsibilities that come with being a world power. In recent years, France has contributed significant numbers of troops to peacekeeping missions in trouble spots like Bosnia and Rwanda, and in 1995 it announced its intention to rejoin the North Atlantic Treaty Organization's military committee, from which it withdrew in 1966. Because France is the world's third largest nuclear power, it must inevitably be involved with questions of nuclear security, but it has encountered considerable international opposition to its nuclear testing. When France briefly resumed nuclear tests in 1995, after a three-year international moratorium, there were outcries from around the globe.

The French republic has been a generous donor of foreign aid to developing countries, and it remains a major trading partner for its former colonies in Africa. But the growing pains experienced by some of these nations, most notably Algeria, have spilled over into France's internal politics, with terrorist attacks in French cities and a backlash of anti-foreigner actions.

Also affecting France's role in the world are its overseas territories (New Caledonia, French Polynesia, French Southern and Antarctic Lands, Wallis and Futuna Islands, St. Pierre and Miquelon, and Mayotte) and its overseas departments (Martinique, Guadeloupe, French Guiana, and Réunion). Inhabitants of the departments, un-

*The ruins of the Château Gaillard lie in a fertile valley in Normandy. The French have cultivated their land for centuries, and today France provides more agricultural products than any other Western European nation.*

*The design of the Pompidou Center in Paris—a building dedicated to cultural and artistic events—suggests the inventiveness of French culture. But many French people worry about losing their distinctive identity as France becomes more closely integrated with the rest of Europe.*

like those of the territories, are French citizens, eligible to vote in French elections.

Perhaps the greatest issue now facing France is its membership in the European Union and the degree to which the French are prepared to sacrifice some of their historic independence to the shared needs of a united Europe. Like its neighbors, France faces daunting challenges in meeting the 1992 Maastricht Treaty's fiscal targets for the introduction of a single European currency. Many French citizens are unhappy with the fiscal restraints demanded of their country, and they are worried that cherished aspects of French culture may be imperiled by the growing integration of Europe.

Nevertheless, the benefits of economic union in Europe are already being seen in increased tourism across national borders and in the strengthening of France's competitiveness in world markets through trans-European business enterprises. Many experts believe the question is no longer whether but when successive phases of European cooperation will enlarge France's role on the world stage.

*A small village lies nestled at the base of the French Alps near Chamonix on a road to Switzerland. Some of France's most beautiful scenery is found in its alpine region.*

# The Land

Lying about as far north of the equator as the state of Maine in the northeastern United States, France occupies part of the extreme west of the European continent. The country, the largest in Western Europe, is bounded on the north by the English Channel; on the northeast by Belgium and Luxembourg; on the east by Germany, Switzerland, and Italy; on the south by the Mediterranean Sea, Spain, and Andorra; and on the west by the Bay of Biscay.

Roughly pentagonal in shape, France covers a land area of 213,010 square miles (553,826 square kilometers). This includes the Mediterranean island of Corsica (its area is 3,367 square miles or 8,754 square kilometers), which is southeast of the mainland. The country's maximum length is about 620 miles (998 kilometers) from the city of Dunkerque on the north coast to the Pyrenees Mountains in the southwest; its greatest width, from the western tip of Brittany to the Rhine River, is approximately the same distance.

The French republic's position and topography have many advantages. It is the only country in Europe, except Spain, that has coastlines on both the Atlantic and the Mediterranean. In France's case, these coasts are mainly bordered by lowlands, making it easy for people and goods to move between the interior of the country and the sea. The Gulf of Lyons on the western side of the Mediterranean Basin gives a convenient approach to two important river routes, the Rhône leading north to the Paris Basin and the Garonne leading northwest to the Aquitaine Basin. (A basin consists of the entire land area drained by a river and its complex of tributary streams.) In the north, France has direct access to the North Sea, a significant international water route.

About half of the country's surface consists of lowlands; the other half is hilly or mountainous. Lowland valleys and plains, scattered with hills and plateaus, run from the Belgian border in the north to the Pyrenees Mountains in the south. The French Alps, the largest and highest mountain area, is located in the southeast. The highest peaks exceed 10,000 feet (3,000 meters). Mont Blanc, rising to 15,781 feet (4,734 meters), is the highest point in France and in all of Europe. France's other mountain ranges are the Massif Central, located in the southeast-central part of the country; the Jura, in the east; the Vosges, in the northeast; and the Pyrenees, on the Spanish border.

The Massif Central, an area of relatively low, rounded mountains, covers approximately one-sixth of the country. The central area of this mountain range is covered by volcanic soil, which is good for both farming and livestock raising. At the core of the Massif Central is an extensive and fertile plateau.

France may be divided into six geographic regions: the Northern Region, the Paris Basin, Normandy, Brittany, the Lower Loire, and the Southwestern Plains. Each region has distinctive landscapes and physical characteristics.

The Northern Region includes the Flanders plain, part of Ardennes, and Lorraine. The Flanders plain stretches southeast from the North Sea coast, which is low and fringed by sand dunes. Farther inland is a rich agricultural region linked to the ports of Calais and Dunkerque by canals. In the center of the Northern Region, the

Flanders plain runs into the foothills of Ardennes, a plateau covered with forests and moors (open, rolling grasslands) growing on peat and clay. The Ardennes plateau continues across the border in Belgium. Lorraine is the eastern part of the Northern Region, tucked into the corner formed by the border with Germany.

The lowlands of France are generally fertile, which accounts in large part for the country's superiority in agriculture. Chief among the lowland areas is the Paris Basin, which is located in the north and center of the country. The basin covers 42,471 square miles (110,000 square kilometers)—about one-fifth of France. Most of this region is covered with a deep layer of *limon*, or loess (rich, fine-grained soil), which is especially good for growing cereals and root crops such as potatoes. Forests, livestock pastures, orchards, wheat fields, and marshes are typical landscapes of this region.

Normandy, on the English Channel coast, is divided into Haute (high) Normandie, north of the Seine River, and Basse (low) Normandie, south of the Seine. The coast of Haute Normandie is dotted with flourishing ports, such as Dieppe and Le Havre, and fishing towns. Basse Normandie is a much larger area. Its eastern plains are widely covered with limon, which makes it an important farming

*Mont Blanc, the highest mountain in France, has long attracted hikers.*

*The rocky coast of Brittany in northwest France is dotted with harbors and ports. Bretons, as the people of Brittany are called, brave the unpredictable weather of the English Channel to earn a living from the sea.*

district; western Normandy is better suited to raising cattle and horses. Forests cover large parts of the area.

West of Normandy is Brittany, a peninsula jutting out into the English Channel. The Country of the Sea, as the coastal part of Brittany is called, is a rugged, rocky coastline with hundreds of tiny bays and numerous small ports. The Country of the Woods, or the interior of the peninsula, is an area of fertile soil, mixed with moorland and wooded areas, where farming flourishes.

South of Normandy and Brittany is the Lower Loire Region, the areas watered by the Loire River and its tributaries. Maine, a district east of Brittany, is primarily wooded and fertile. South of Maine, the inland districts of Anjou and Touraine have a climate and soil that favor grapevines and fruits. A district called the Vendée, along the coast south of the city of Nantes, is sandy and barren.

The Southwestern Plains Region covers approximately one-seventh of France. It stretches from the Massif Central in the east to the Bay of Biscay in the west. Its south border is the Pyrenees Mountains. This region is agricultural, probably best known for the Bordeaux wine communes in the Médoc district near the coast. Farther inland is the Aquitaine Basin, with some of France's richest soil and most productive agricultural areas.

In addition to France itself, the French republic includes ten overseas holdings. Four of them are departments and six are territories or so-called territorial collectivities. The departments are Guadeloupe and Martinique in the Caribbean, French Guiana in South America, and Réunion in the Indian Ocean. France's territorial holdings are New Caledonia, French Polynesia, Wallis and Futuna Islands, St. Pierre and Miquelon, Mayotte, and the French Southern and Antarctic Lands located in the Indian Ocean and Antarctica.

Although France has more than 200 navigable streams with a total length of 5,500 miles (8,855 kilometers), there are only 4 large rivers. The Garonne rises in the Pyrenees and follows a northwestern course to the Bay of Biscay, where it empties into a large inlet at Bordeaux. The Rhône River originates far up in the Vosges Mountains and flows south to the Mediterranean. The Seine rises in the east, wends its way in a northwest direction through Paris, and eventually empties into the English Channel. The Loire starts as a small stream in the Massif Central, flows northwest to Orléans, then suddenly veers to the west and enters the Bay of Biscay at Nantes.

# Climate and Weather

France has a temperate climate, with seasons similar to those in the United States. The Gulf Stream, a warm Atlantic Ocean current, keeps the temperature moderate. The country has four types of climate. In the western regions near the ocean there is moderate rainfall, mostly during the winter, and temperature changes are not dramatic. Most of the inland part of the country has significant seasonal temperature changes and heavier summer rainfall. The Mediterranean coast has hot, dry summers and mild, wet winters.

The mountain regions have cool summers and cold, sunny winters. No part of France is free from frost or snow except the most sheltered areas on the Mediterranean.

Bordeaux, near the west coast, is an example of a city that experiences the western oceanic climate. Here the average January temperature is 40° Fahrenheit (4° Celsius) and the average August temperature is 68° Fahrenheit (20° Celsius). In the higher areas of the central and eastern parts of the country, the mean winter temperature is below freezing—in Strasbourg, the January temperature averages 32° Fahrenheit (0° Celsius), and for August the average is 64° Fahrenheit (18° Celsius). The Mediterranean coast, sheltered by the protecting mountains to the north, is a paradise for vacationers. Marseilles basks in Mediterranean mildness, with an average winter temperature of 45° Fahrenheit (7° Celsius); summer in Marseilles is warmer than in the rest of France, with the temperature in August at around 72° Fahrenheit (22° Celsius).

Rainfall is particularly heavy in the mountainous areas (more than 55 inches, or 140 centimeters, annually). The nearby hills and plateaus receive 31 inches (79 centimeters) to 35 inches (89 centimeters) each year. Along the Mediterranean and farther inland, the average annual rainfall is 25 inches (63 centimeters).

# Plant and Animal Life

France's plant life can be divided into four geographic types: continental in the northern and central regions, oceanic along the Atlantic coast, Mediterranean along the southern coast, and alpine in the mountainous areas.

The continental type consists mainly of oak and beech forests throughout the drier parts of the north and central areas and on the upper slopes of the valleys of the Oise and lower Seine rivers. Marshes are common in the low-lying areas, particularly in the valley of the lower Loire and the plain between the Massif Central and the Loire.

Part of this area has been planted with pine, birch, and oak. Along the western border are stretches of marsh where willows and poplar trees grow.

Along the Atlantic coast willows and bog myrtle (evergreen shrubs) grow in the wetter areas, and stunted oak trees spread through the drier areas. The highlands of Brittany are characterized by expanses of moor and scrub (land covered with small, stunted trees and bushes). South of Bordeaux, the swamps beyond the coastal sand dunes have been drained and reforested with pine.

On the Mediterranean coast in the south olive, mulberry, and fig trees and flowering vines, grapevines, and strawberry plants are common. Fields of herbs, including lavender, thyme, rosemary, and others, thrive in this area. Along the Gulf of Lyons the inhabitants grow olives, mulberries, and vines. The eastern half of the Pyrenees bears forests of oak and Spanish chestnut; the western half supports forests of ash and beech on the lower slopes.

Alpine plants flourish below the snow line of the Alps. Below the cushion pine and mosses of the upper altitudes are flowering plants, including dwarf pine and juniper. Lower still is a continuous belt of evergreen conifers, followed by beeches and oaks on the bottom slopes. Large areas of forest in the Alps have been turned into pastures.

About 90 species of mammals are native to France. The largest is the brown bear, which is still common in the Pyrenees, although in the Alps it is found only in remote forests. Other woodland inhabitants include polecats, wildcats, wild boars, and roe deer. The commonest mammals in the country are hedgehogs, moles, bats, foxes, weasels, squirrels, and rabbits. Badgers are found throughout France, hares mainly in the northeast.

*Vercingetorix succeeded in uniting several tribes in Gaul (as France was known in the 1st century B.C.) but failed to repel the invading Roman army led by Julius Caesar. This engraving depicts his surrender to Caesar.*

# Before the Revolution

The earliest-recorded inhabitants of the territory that is now France—in about 600 B.C.—were the Ligurians and the Celts or Gauls. The Ligurians, who tended to be short, slender, and dark, occupied the area south of the central plateau. The Gauls, a tall, blond race, came from beyond the Rhine River, which separates present-day France from Germany. The Gauls occupied the rest of the country—known as Gaul at this time—along with other Germanic peoples in the east. The separate tribes of Gauls never achieved a central government. They managed to unite only in a vain effort to repel the invading Romans.

In 52 B.C. Gaul fell to the Roman army led by Julius Caesar. Under Roman domination, the country advanced rapidly, numerous towns sprang up, and civilization flourished. Over four centuries, the shared Latin language, policy, religion, and administration unified Gaul, which prospered under the Romans.

During the 5th century A.D. the German tribes of the Visigoths, Burgundians, and Franks gradually migrated to Gaul. The Visigoths established a powerful kingdom in Aquitaine in the southwest, the Burgundians settled in the eastern region now known as Burgundy, and the Franks remained in the northeast around Paris. Toward the end of the 5th century, as the Roman Empire weakened and disintegrated, the Franks, under a leader named Clovis, drove out the Romans and took the land for themselves. It is from the Franks that France gets its name.

Clovis set himself up as ruler not only of much of Gaul but also of large areas east of the Rhine. He understood well the strength of the Christian church in Gaul. By converting to Christianity, Clovis laid the foundation for a unified state. His conquests took on the character of holy wars. Backed by the church, he conquered most of Gaul, assassinating the kings of neighboring tribes that refused to convert to Christianity. The dynasty, or line of rulers, established by Clovis is known as the Merovingian dynasty; it lasted for two and a half centuries.

*Clovis, who ended Roman domination in Gaul in 486, is said to have promised to become a Christian in return for victory in battle.*

Clovis died in 511, leaving his dominions to be divided among his four sons as the four kingdoms of Reims, Paris, Orléans, and Soissons. For 50 years Clovis's heirs sought to continue his work and add to their dominions. From 523 to 532 they subdued Burgundy and the southeastern region of Provence. They even attempted to conquer Italy, Spain, and Germany. The last Merovingian kings were ineffective rulers. Real power was in the hands of their palace mayors. One of these officials, Pippin the Short, took the throne in 751 as the first king of the Carolingian dynasty.

Pippin's son, Charles the Great, or Charlemagne, succeeded him in about 770. Charlemagne proved to be one of the greatest rulers in European history. Under his reign, the empire spread from Denmark to the Pyrenees and Italy and from Brittany to Austria. In 800 Charlemagne was crowned the first Holy Roman Emperor by the pope.

Although he was practically illiterate, Charlemagne enthusiastically supported education and established schools throughout the land. During his reign, literature and the arts flourished. He divided his kingdom into districts, appointing an official to run each. Justice was administered by men who traveled over the domain in pairs. Charlemagne reorganized the laws and gave the people a better government than they had had before. At his death, in 814, he was succeeded by his only surviving son, Louis the Pious.

Under Louis's reign, the empire gradually crumbled. It was divided among his sons by the Treaty of Verdun in 843. Under the treaty, Charles the Bald received the portion that became known as France. Under the last Carolingian kings, France lived through a century of anarchy. The disorder in this period was in large part due to raiders from Scandinavia, today known as Vikings. In 987 Hugh Capet, another ambitious palace official, was proclaimed king and began to restore order. With him began the Capetian dynasty, which was to reign for 800 years.

Louis IX (Saint Louis) was one of the most famous of the Capetian kings. During his reign (1226–70), France enjoyed a preeminence that made the 13th century one of the most important periods in its history. Louis IX managed to achieve a balance among the powers of that time—royalty, the church, the aristocracy, and the town councils. French architects and skilled craftsmen of the period built Gothic cathedrals and monuments whose beauty and majestic proportions still endure and astonish.

Louis IX himself led the final two crusades against the Muslims, or Saracens, as they were called then. The Crusades, which were undertaken by the people of Europe from 1096 to 1270, were a series of religious expeditions to free Jerusalem from Muslim rule. The Crusades did not succeed in liberating Jerusalem, but they increased the power of the Christian church, providing a unifying bond for all Europe. During the final crusade, in 1270, Louis died of a plague in North Africa; he was made a saint by the pope in 1297.

The ruling families of England and France were connected by marriages and complicated lines of descent and inheritance. The two nations had long quarreled about supremacy in France; finally, in 1337, there began a series of wars that lasted on and off for more than a century. The wars were collectively known as the Hundred Years' War.

The trouble began when Edward III of England claimed to be king of France because his mother was a sister of King Charles IV of France. But Philip VI, a cousin of Charles, was crowned instead. At Crécy, in 1346, the first great battle of the war was fought. England emerged victorious. Ten years later the English won another great victory at Poitiers. But the English were never able to hold for long the ground they won, and the French had driven them out before Charles VI succeeded to the throne. War was resumed in 1415, when England was again victorious, winning the Battle of

*After Charlemagne conquered much of western Europe, Pope Leo III crowned him emperor on Christmas Day, 800. Charlemagne's Carolingian Empire did not survive his death, but one-fourth went to his grandson Charles the Bald and became the land now known as France.*

Agincourt. Five years later, by the Treaty of Troyes, Henry V of England forced Charles VI to name him heir to the French throne.

By 1428 the Hundred Years' War had ruined the French countryside; areas that once had flourished were wastelands. It was at this time, when England possessed most of France, that Joan of Arc, a young peasant girl, arose to inspire the French to overcome the English.

Of all the women in history who have influenced the course of nations, hardly any compares with Joan of Arc. She was born in the little peasant town of Domrémy in 1412. As a child she was filled with the desire to help her country, but it was not until 1428, when the English were besieging the city of Orléans, that she experienced powerful religious visions that told her what to do. Fired with the

A wall mural in the Panthéon portrays Joan of Arc about to be burned at the stake by the English, who hated her for leading French armies to victory against them. The English sentenced her to death for being a witch; the Roman Catholic church declared her a saint.

belief that God had entrusted her with the mission of saving France, she approached King Charles to tell him of her dreams. She was thought to be insane, for it seemed preposterous that a girl of 17 could do anything to save the city, much less the entire nation.

But Joan prevailed on the king, and finally she was allowed to ride out at the head of the army toward Orléans. She was an inspiring sight for the war-weary men. Clad in shining armor, with her long locks falling over her shoulders, she held aloft the banner of France and a gleaming sword. She was successful in her first battles. In May 1429 the English were driven from Orléans, and the city hailed Joan as its deliverer.

The English still held a large part of France, including Paris, and Joan next launched an attack on that city. Here she was unsuccessful, but in spite of a wound, she fought on. Finally, in May 1430 she was captured by the Burgundians and sold to the English. Joan was put on trial by the English, who found her guilty of being a witch. In May 1431 she was burned at the stake in the streets of Rouen: a fire that blazed her name through history.

Putting her to death was a mistake for the English. She had united the French, and her name spread through the land as a symbol of courage and patriotism—traits that her people have cherished ever since. When the French heard of her death, they vowed vengeance and fought with increased zeal. By 1453 the English had been driven from French soil, and a united French nation arose. The Hundred Years' War had come to an end.

In 1456 Joan of Arc was cleared of all charges of witchcraft by the church, and in 1919 she was declared a saint by the pope. Today, she is one of the most revered saints of Roman Catholicism.

At the end of the Hundred Years' War, France's rulers continued their slow and patient work of strengthening the kingdom. Louis XI, who ruled from 1461 to 1483, was the first to organize his kingdom as a modern state. He developed the shipping trade, established the silk and wool industries, and encouraged a stable currency. His reign marked the end, in France, of the Middle Ages—the period in history generally falling between ancient and modern civilizations, or between the 5th and the 15th centuries.

Once it had recovered from the Hundred Years' War and was well into the process of rebuilding, France was again plunged into a violent struggle—this time of a religious nature—in the mid-16th century. The Wars of Religion were waged by the Catholics against the Huguenots, the people of France who adopted the Protestant religion, which developed from the teachings of Martin Luther in the German states in the first decades of the 1500s. Although the Huguenots were a small minority, the Catholic nobility saw their increasing political power as a threat. Thus began the persecution of the Protestants, resulting in the massacre of many of them in August 1572 on St. Bartholomew's Day. King Henry IV of France, who was sympathetic to the Huguenots, issued the Edict of Nantes in 1598. It granted civil and religious liberties to the Protestants and brought about a temporary peace between the warring religions.

Henry IV's son, Louis XIII, became king in 1610 at the age of nine. The most significant undertaking of Louis's reign was the relentless war carried on against the Huguenots. But Louis XIII was not the main force in the suppression of the Protestants. He was influenced—and some history books say controlled—by his prime minister, Cardinal Richelieu.

No royal crown ever adorned the head of Cardinal Richelieu, yet he was the virtual ruler of France from 1624 to his death in 1642. Richelieu gained power in the church and the government simultaneously. Under his direction, France gained the strongest position it had ever had in world affairs. He encouraged French expansion overseas and directed missionaries who founded Montreal in Canada. He established colonies in Senegal in western Africa and at Fort-Dauphin in Madagascar. Richelieu was also responsible for establishing colonies in Martinique and Guadeloupe in the Caribbean and Guiana in South America.

In 1643 Louis XIV succeeded his father as king of France. His reign, which lasted 72 years—the longest in the history of Europe— marked one of the most splendid as well as one of the most unfortunate periods in French history. France grew rapidly during the first half of Louis's reign. But many historians attribute this growth to the efforts of Jean-Baptiste Colbert, Louis's minister of state and secretary for the navy, who was responsible for the external and internal administration of the kingdom.

Colbert was ambitious and hardworking. His economic measures were responsible for France's initial development as a commercial and industrial nation. He set up many factories, built roads

*The St. Bartholomew's Day massacre on August 24, 1572, occurred on the eve of the wedding of Henry of Navarre, a Huguenot leader. Henry of Navarre became King Henry IV in 1589, converted to Catholicism in 1593, and issued the Edict of Nantes, which granted religious freedom to Huguenots, in 1598.*

and canals, and instituted a system of import taxes that meant that manufactured goods brought into France were taxed, whereas raw materials could be brought in free—a powerful encouragement to the French to manufacture their own goods. Colbert also had ships built and encouraged exports. France grew in territory as well as economically during Colbert's administration. He increased the country's colonies in Canada and gave financial support to Cavelier de La Salle's colonization of Louisiana (named after Louis XIV).

Colbert died in 1683. His achievements were eroded by the Sun King (the name Louis XIV adopted) during the next 32 years. Louis frittered away France's resources on extravagances designed to display his majestic style. He moved his court to Versailles, 12 miles (19.2 kilometers) outside Paris. There he built Europe's greatest palace. It was reputed to have cost six months' worth of the country's entire income.

*The size and splendor of the palace of Versailles and its gardens were intended by Louis XIV to reflect the power and glory of the French monarchy. The staggering cost of the palace marked the beginning of 75 years of wasteful spending that led to the monarchy's destruction in the French Revolution.*

Historians have condemned Louis XIV for his great misjudgment concerning the Huguenots. The Sun King, a devout Catholic, revoked the Edict of Nantes in 1685 and resumed the persecution of the Protestants. The Huguenots—many of whom were business and industrial leaders—thereupon began to leave the country. Half a million of them left, most settling in America. Louis also provoked costly conflict with neighboring nations in the name of extending France's borders, thus further diminishing the country's assets. To finance his expansion plans and his grand way of life, the Sun King inflicted huge taxes on his subjects. This crushed the poorer classes and ruined industries. Louis XIV's mismanagement sparked the flames of the revolution that arrived 75 years later. He died in 1715, having ruined a kingdom that had just begun to thrive. His funeral was marked by the rejoicing of the people.

The reign of Louis XIV was not just one of wasteful spending. In the 17th century French literature reached a peak, especially in the works of three dramatists. This was the age of Molière (1622–73), whose comedies are masterpieces of wit and satire; of Corneille (1606–84), called the creator of French tragedy; and of Racine (1639–99), whose tragedies are still regarded as perfect poetic expression. To his credit, Louis did encourage the arts to flourish— in keeping with his love of the good life. His chief legacy is Europe's "Palace of Palaces" that he built at Versailles.

The extravagances of Louis XIV were continued by his great-grandson, Louis XV, who succeeded him in 1715. His rule was highlighted by expensive wars with Austria and England. Some wars against the English took place on American soil and are known as the French and Indian Wars because France was allied with Native American tribes. During the French and Indian Wars, France lost most of its holdings in North America. At the death of Louis XV in 1774, French power and prestige were at a low ebb, and the nation's resources were greatly diminished. The weak but well-meaning Louis

*Hordes of Parisians, enraged by Louis XVI's indecisive response to the National Assembly's demands, stormed the Bastille on July 14, 1789. Although they freed only the seven inmates of the royal prison that day, their action began the Revolution that eventually freed France from the ancien régime.*

XVI, who came next to the throne, would pay for the excesses of his two predecessors.

In 1787, with the treasury empty, Louis XVI decided that France's "privileged" class—the nobles and the clergy—should pay taxes just like the "unprivileged" class—the Third Estate, or commoners. The nobles and the clergy refused to do so, demanding instead that a meeting of the Estates General be called to discuss and solve France's economic problems. The Estates General was a body with representatives from the three classes, or estates: the clergy, the nobles, and the Third Estate, which now included a growing force of the middle class, or bourgeoisie.

On May 5, 1789, the Estates General met at Versailles. The three estates' representatives had always met and voted in separate rooms, and the privileged classes outvoted the unprivileged by two to one. However, on this occasion the representatives of the Third Estate, who numbered as many as the other two groups of representatives combined, insisted that all meet and vote in the same room. The king refused, and after weeks of separate meetings the Third Estate flatly refused to continue discussions until France was given a constitution.

On June 27, Louis XVI reluctantly yielded to the commoners' demand and ordered the three estates to meet as one assembly for the purpose of giving France a written constitution. Opinion is divided as to why Louis gave in to this demand, which was likely to mean an end to the monarch's power. He was probably simply afraid of the increasing revolutionary sentiment in the country. When it reconvened, the Estates General became known as the National Assembly.

But Louis XVI was again swayed, this time by the nobility and the clergy. They urged the king to dissolve the assembly, and he agreed. At the same time he gathered 30,000 soldiers in and around Paris. On July 11, Louis made a final foolish blunder: He fired his chief minister, Jacques Necker, who was of common birth and considered a symbol of reform within the government. For the people of Paris, this was the final act of betrayal. On July 14, an angry mob in Paris stormed the Bastille, an ancient royal prison, and freed several political prisoners. The French Revolution was under way.

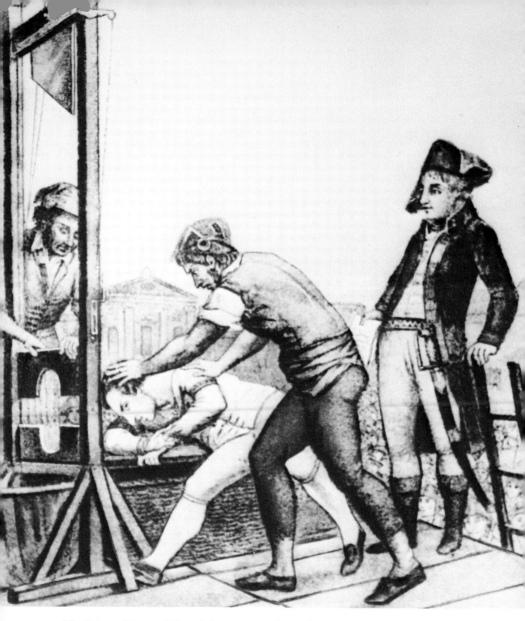

The Reign of Terror followed the opening phase of the French Revolution as zeal for reform turned into fanaticism and violent power struggles. Robespierre, one of the leaders of the Reign of Terror, was sent to the guillotine by his rivals. When he was in power, he had condemned many to the same fate.

# The Revolution
# and After

In addition to the oppression and the disillusionment suffered by France's masses, another important factor contributed to the people's overthrow of the Bastille. French writers and philosophers—particularly Voltaire (1694–1778) and Jean-Jacques Rousseau (1712–78)—had published books and stories pointing out the injustices of the French monarchy and the superiority of representative government. Students read these books and passed on the ideas in them to others not so well educated. Groups of workers and peasants gathered to discuss matters and plan some remedy.

Voltaire and Rousseau were two of the main spokesmen of what is called the Age of Enlightenment, which corresponded roughly to the 18th century in Europe. Thinkers of the Enlightenment stressed the right of individuals to determine their own destiny. From 1760 to 1789 Enlightenment ideas percolated through popular thought and discussion throughout France until the souls of common folk were fired with the desire for Liberty, Equality, and Fraternity—the watchwords of the Revolution.

After the revolt on July 14, the king made no serious effort to suppress the rebels. The citizens of Paris, taking the initiative, organized a government for the city. It was supported by a citizen militia called the National Guard. Louis XVI again yielded, promising to remove his troops and to approve the Paris government.

Inspired by the successful revolt in Paris, the starving peasants of France decided to follow suit. Groups armed with pitchforks, scythes, or whatever weapons they could lay their hands on began attacking castles and manor houses of the nobles. They demanded that rents and taxes be abolished.

On August 4, the National Assembly met. Fearful of a general insurrection, the assembly decided that some concessions must be made to the peasants of France. After a night of debate, the representatives decreed that the ancien régime, or old system, was abolished. In other words, the privileges of the monarchy, the nobles, and the clergy had ended.

Three weeks later, on August 26, the Declaration of the Rights of Man and of the Citizen was formulated. This declaration, which became the beginning of the constitution, affirmed that "the principle of all sovereignty lies essentially in the nation; no individual or corporation can exercise authority which does not expressly emanate from it." On the political level, the declaration put an end to royal rule by divine right and guaranteed rights of representation and equality before the law. It asserted that "law is the expression of the general will" and recognized "freedom of the individual, freedom of conscience, freedom of speech, and freedom to write and to assemble, and the inviolability of property."

Louis XVI would not agree to the declaration, especially to the part that dealt with the abolition of "royalty by divine right." Once more he gave way to the nobles and the clergy and summoned his army to Versailles in an effort to quell the rebellion.

On October 5, a procession of Parisian women, followed by detachments of the National Guard, set out for Versailles. They were short of food, and their aim was to force the king to give them bread and to demand his acceptance of the declaration passed by the National Assembly. Early the next morning, the women stormed the palace, captured King Louis XVI and his queen, Marie-Antoinette, and took them back to Paris as prisoners.

The next two years were the quietest period in the whole revolutionary decade. During this time, the National Assembly set about the tasks of cleaning up the country's messy economic situation and drafting a constitution, which was completed in September 1791. The National Assembly then dissolved itself, and a newly elected Legislative Assembly, as provided for in the constitution, was convened.

In 1792 Austria and Prussia went to war with France. After initial defeats of the French army, riots broke out in Paris. In September the National Convention was elected to replace the Legislative Assembly. The convention unanimously decreed that monarchy was forever abolished in France. On September 21, the First Republic of France was proclaimed. Meanwhile, the advance of the Prussian

*Approximately 6,000 women, angered by food shortages in Paris, marched to Versailles on October 6, 1789, captured the royal family, and brought them to Paris.*

army had been checked, and soon afterward the Austrians were driven back. By the end of 1792 the French armies were victorious.

Intoxicated by their success, the National Convention passed a decree announcing that the French armies would gladly come to the aid of all peoples who wished to free themselves from the tyranny of kings and nobles. Soon after, in January 1793, Louis XVI was put on trial, found guilty, and sentenced to death by guillotine—a device used for execution by beheading.

The execution of Louis and the fear that France's armies might bring revolution to other countries convinced Europe's rulers that all monarchies were in danger. The rulers of Great Britain, Holland, Spain, Portugal, Sweden, Naples, Sardinia, Austria, and Prussia decided to unite to suppress the French Revolution. They wanted to dissolve the National Convention and restore the monarchy in France.

Such powerful military opposition would appear to have been too much for any one nation. But the allies lacked unity, whereas

*Marie-Antoinette went to the guillotine on October 16, 1793. Superficially polite to the end, she apologized to the executioner for stepping on his foot.*

the French were fighting in defense of their homeland and for a cause in which they believed. Nationalism proved a decisive factor for the Republic. The entire country mobilized to repel the enemies. At first, the allied nations of Europe were successful in the struggle, but by mid-1795 the French had managed to push the foreign armies out of France. The Republic had saved its revolution.

# Reign of Terror

While the French were engaged in the struggle against the foreign invaders, the country was also undergoing one of the bloodiest periods in its history—the Reign of Terror. In the summer of 1793 the Jacobins, an extreme prorevolutionary group within the National Convention, controlled the country. Led by two of the most important leaders of the Revolution—Georges-Jacques Danton and Maximilien Robespierre—the Jacobins searched out and punished anyone suspected of opposing the Revolution. A new court, the Revolutionary Tribunal, was created to deal with suspects; the guillotine became the chief implement of execution.

Between March 1793 and July 1794 the tribunal tried and condemned to death about 2,600 persons. Another 17,000 lost their life when revolts in the provinces were crushed. Queen Marie-Antoinette and her court were among the first to lose their head. Many of the condemned were really enemies of the Revolution; some, however, had never taken part in politics but were unfortunate enough to be denounced by malicious neighbors. Innocent or guilty, they were herded into prisons, brought before the tribunal, then carried in carts through crowded streets to the guillotine.

As the slaughter continued, Danton, one of the more moderate Jacobins, urged a lessening of the violence. The fanatical Robespierre had him declared a traitor, and Danton was executed in April 1794. For three months longer, Robespierre remained the outstanding figure in the National Convention. During this time he escalated the Reign of Terror in order to establish his idea of a "Reign of Virtue." Eventually, when the people could take no more bloodshed, the convention decreed the arrest of Robespierre. He was guillotined on July 27, 1794. The Reign of Terror had ended.

# Napoléon

It was during France's struggle to defend the Revolution against the coalition of foreign nations that Napoléon Bonaparte first won recognition. In 1793, at age 24, he led a French army to defeat the English at the city of Toulon. In 1795 he was called to Paris to quell an uprising. Because of his military successes, Napoléon was placed in command of the French army in Italy, where he won some important victories. By 1798, after he defeated Austria and invaded Egypt, he was hailed as a military genius.

Returning to France from Egypt in October 1799, Napoléon was a hero. The government at this time—known as the Directory—was far from stable. France's finances were again in a muddle. The people, tired of bloodshed, poverty, and unrest, were seeking a strong, capable government. Napoléon seized the initiative. In November he overthrew the Directory and named himself first consul of the French Republic. This event marked the end of the French Revolution.

The first consul at once exhibited his talent for efficient administration. He appointed administrators called prefects, who soon established orderly government where confusion had existed under the Directory. A new and stable currency replaced the worthless paper money that had formerly circulated. New taxes, heavy but reasonably just and honestly collected, restored the credit of the government by providing an adequate revenue.

In 1802 Napoléon selected consul for life as his new title. The title was approved by the populace in a landslide vote. Two years

*One of the greatest military geniuses in history, Napoléon Bonaparte conquered most of western Europe by the age of 39. This painting depicts the Battle of Arcole, one of his early victories, which took place while he commanded the French republican army in Italy in 1796–97.*

later, he asked the people to permit him to take the title of emperor. This they also approved by an overwhelming majority.

But Napoléon was not content with his successes in France. He was determined to conquer and rule all of Europe. In 1811 the emperor, at the height of his power, controlled most of western Europe—with the notable exception of England. In 1813 England, Prussia, Austria, and Russia formed an alliance to crush the conqueror. Their allied armies eventually overcame Napoléon's forces, and he was forced to abdicate, or give up the throne, in 1814. This was not the end of the emperor, however. He retired to the island of Elba, off the coast of Italy, and plotted his return.

The monarchy was immediately restored in France. Louis XVIII, a brother of Louis XVI, was proclaimed king. The foreign alliance and King Louis then signed the Treaty of Paris, which returned the lands conquered by Napoléon to their former owners.

On March 1, 1815, Napoléon returned to France. Together with some faithful followers he marched to Paris and overthrew Louis XVIII. For 100 days Napoléon again ruled in France. Once more he had to contend with allied forces determined to dislodge him. On June 18, he was finally crushed by the British general Wellington in the Battle of Waterloo in Belgium. Napoléon was banished forever to the island of St. Helena in the Atlantic Ocean. There he was carefully guarded by the English until his death in 1821.

## Return to Monarchy

In July 1815 Louis XVIII was restored to the throne. At first he was supported by the common people. But the aristocrats who had fled the country when the Revolution began soon returned and resumed their suppression of the peasantry. Louis ruled until his death in 1824. He was succeeded by his brother, Charles X.

Although Charles X had taken an oath to uphold reforms instituted by Napoléon, it soon became clear that he intended to restore the ancien régime. The people's discontent increased to bitter opposition and led to another revolution in July 1830. Parisians threw up barricades in the streets and fought the king's soldiers. Charles abdicated, and the duke of Orléans, Louis Philippe, replaced him— he was known as the Citizen King.

King Louis Philippe's reign was unpopular with all classes. By the early 1840s his lax government and inactivity caused increasing dissatisfaction. Many upper-middle-class members of the moderate faction demanded that the right to vote be given to more people.

The lower-middle-class Republicans still hoped to see a democratic republic established in France. But Louis Philippe refused all efforts at reform.

In February 1848 Parisians again revolted. The king's troops made little effort to suppress the uprising. Louis Philippe became frightened and fled the city. The revolutionaries then proclaimed France a republic once more and formed a temporary government consisting of five Republicans and four Socialists (advocates of socialism, an economic and social system in which the means of producing and distributing goods are owned and controlled by the state). This temporary government called for the election of a National Assembly to draft a new constitution for France. The election brought mainly middle-class representatives, or members of the class called the bourgeoisie, to the assembly. The Socialists of the lowest classes violently objected to their lack of representation. The bourgeoisie, now thoroughly frightened of the Socialists, organized an army to support the National Assembly. In June, 1,500 Socialists were killed in 4 days' fighting in the streets of Paris.

## Second Republic, Second Empire

The National Assembly then drafted a new constitution for France. It provided for a president and a legislative assembly, both to be elected by male voters. France now entered the Second Republic. Elections were held in December 1848 and May 1849. By this time, the "bloody June days" had frightened people all over France, and fear of socialism made people suspicious even of a republican government. The result was that the majority of men elected to the assembly were not in favor of a republic.

The man elected as president of the Republic was Louis-Napoléon, nephew of Napoléon Bonaparte. According to the constitution, the president would occupy office for four years. But Louis-Napoléon's great aim was to restore the empire. By the end of his third year as president, he had his term extended to an additional 10 years; in 1852 he was declared Emperor Napoléon III. France then entered the period called the Second Empire.

During the first 10 years of Napoléon III's reign the people of France were generally contented. The emperor brought economic prosperity to the nation. He undertook public works projects, beautified and modernized Paris, and built new roads and railroads. In foreign affairs, Napoléon III allied France with England and Turkey in the Crimean War against Russia; and in 1859 he sided with Italy in a war against Austria. These moves increased his popularity at home and abroad.

*Napoléon III, a nephew of Napoléon Bonaparte, was elected president of France in 1848. After proclaiming himself and his wife, Eugénie, emperor and empress in 1852, he ruled France under the Second Empire until he was captured in the Franco-Prussian War in 1870.*

Between 1860 and 1870, however, republican sentiment grew again as a result of Napoléon III's blunders in foreign policy. From 1862 to 1867 he had tried to establish an empire in Mexico, but he was forced to abandon the enterprise when the United States protested. The worst blunder, however, was the Franco-Prussian War, or War of 1870. It brought about the downfall of Napoléon III and the end of the Second Empire.

The war was a disaster for France. The country was thoroughly defeated, and in 1871 Paris was controlled by the Germans. A National Assembly was then elected by the French to arrange peace terms with the Germans. According to the peace treaty signed in May 1871, France had to give up the provinces of Alsace and Lorraine to Germany; France also had to pay an indemnity to Germany amounting to U.S. $1 billion, which it took 3 years to do.

# Third Republic

The chief problem now was to decide which form of government would be adopted by France—monarchy or republic? The National Assembly was divided into two main camps. The Republicans wished to establish a democratic republic; the Orléanists wanted to restore the Orléanist monarchy or return descendants of Louis Philippe to the throne. Until the conflict was resolved, a constitution could not be adopted.

From 1871 to 1873 the National Assembly governed France without even trying to write a constitution. The government was directed by Louis-Adolphe Thiers—one of the leaders in the peace talks with Germany—as president. Thiers was assisted by a ministry composed of Republicans and Orléanists. Finally, in 1875 a compromise constitution that seemed to satisfy everyone was drawn up. It provided for a president, a senate, and a chamber of deputies. The chamber represented the democratic element; the senate, the aristocratic element; and the president, the royal element.

France's Third Republic thus resembled a constitutional monarchy. It lasted until 1940, when it was replaced by the Vichy government during the occupation of France by Nazi Germany in World War II.

Toward the end of the 19th century the Third Republic gradually developed a program of overseas expansion and official colonization, starting in Algeria (1848) and Tunisia (1881), continuing in Indochina (1883) and throughout central and equatorial Africa, including Senegal and Madagascar (1895), which it had occupied since the 17th century, and finishing in Morocco (1904). This made France the second largest colonial power, after Britain, and spread the French language around the world.

In the 1890s a scandal involving a Jewish French army officer, Captain Alfred Dreyfus, had serious repercussions for French politics. In 1894 Dreyfus was convicted by a military court of selling important information to the German government. He was sentenced to life imprisonment on Devil's Island, a French prison colony in the Caribbean. Proof of his innocence soon began to mount, however, and the French public became sharply divided over his case. Monarchists, Catholics, and the army believed him guilty. Republicans and Socialists rallied to his defense.

When it was brought to light that the real traitor was Major Ferdinand Walsin Esterhazy and that high-ranking army officers had falsified the evidence convicting Dreyfus, the prisoner was freed. The Dreyfus affair not only discredited monarchists and the army but also strengthened the republican form of government and the French Socialist party, which was formed in 1905.

The Dreyfus affair also demonstrated the extent of anti-Semitism in France. Thus, France's reputation as the most enlightened and liberal country in Europe was greatly weakened. The affair had an effect on the Catholic church—in 1905 the church and state in France were officially separated, and the government no longer paid

*The Dreyfus affair divided French society for 12 years, from 1894 to 1906. The debate over Captain Dreyfus's innocence or guilt raged on in newspapers, magazines, and books until he was finally declared innocent of treason by the French army. This magazine cover depicts Captain Dreyfus being expelled from the army and stripped of his rank and sword.*

the salaries of the Catholic clergy or recognized special privileges for Catholics.

## World War I and Its Aftermath

In 1914 the powers of Europe clashed in the conflagration known as World War I, or the Great War. France was allied with Britain, Russia, Italy, and Japan against the Central Powers of Germany and Austria-Hungary, which were joined by Turkey and Bulgaria. The United States joined the Allies in 1917. The war ended on French soil in September 1918.

The Allies met in Paris in January 1919 to discuss peace terms. Among the measures finally accepted was that Germany would return to France the provinces of Alsace and Lorraine that it had won in the War of 1870. The Treaty of Versailles, setting forth the terms of peace, was signed in June 1919.

France suffered many serious problems as a result of World War I. Almost one and a half million Frenchmen had died on the battlefield. Thousands of homes and factories had been destroyed. The nation was beset by unemployment, inflation, and economic hardship after the war.

The political parties, united in wartime, resumed their traditional conflicts afterward. On one side stood the monarchists and the conservatives; on the other, the radical Republicans, the Socialists, and the Communists. Both sides strove for control of the government during the 1920s and 1930s. Neither would cooperate with the other when the nation was threatened from within by strikes and riots and from without by the revived threat of Germany in the late 1930s.

## France and World War II

The German tanks that roared into Poland on September 1, 1939, marked the beginning of a war that was to last six long, destructive years. The responsibility for this war—World War II—was clear. The rulers of Italy, Germany, and Japan, known collectively as the Axis, desired to expand their territory and influence by force. Adolf Hitler of Germany was the main aggressor. The Axis powers were met in combat by the Allies, mainly Britain, France, Russia, and the United States.

After capturing Poland, Finland, and Belgium, the Germans moved on to France. In June 1940 the Germans took northern France and began their assault on Paris, which fell on June 14. The rapid fall of France astonished the Allies and came as a surprise even to the Axis. Two main factors accounted for the collapse: First, the German armed forces were superior to the French in manpower,

*(continued on p. 65)*

# Scenes of
# FRANCE

◄ *A copy of* The Thinker, *by Auguste Rodin, the greatest sculptor of 19th-century France, stands in the garden outside the Rodin Museum in Paris.*

▼ *Claude Monet, a 19th-century Impressionist, depicted the gardens and ponds of his home at Giverny in many of his later paintings. The house and grounds, including this canal and bridge, have been restored to much the same state as when Monet made them the subject of his work.*

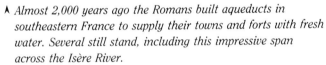
↖ *Almost 2,000 years ago the Romans built aqueducts in southeastern France to supply their towns and forts with fresh water. Several still stand, including this impressive span across the Isère River.*

➤ *In Bordelais, harvesters gather the grapes for wine by hand. Many believe France's wines, which include bordeaux, beaujolais, burgundy, champagne, and numerous others, are the best in the world.*

∨ *The Champ de Mars, formerly a military parade ground in the center of Paris, is today the scene of more peaceful pursuits, such as feeding the pigeons and sparrows on a sunny day.*

▼ *French schoolchildren can take advantage of an excellent educational system. In addition to the free public schools, this predominantly Roman Catholic country has numerous parochial schools staffed by members of religious orders—nuns, monks, and priests.*

▲ *Young Parisians gather for conversation in one of the many cafés that dot the sidewalks of France's capital.*

⋀ *Fresh fruits, vegetables, flowers, and seafood—all the flavorful products of France's farms and waters—are available in the bustling stalls of Les Halles, an open-air market complex in metropolitan Paris.*

◄ *The picturesque neighborhoods and busy street life of Paris have attracted painters for more than a century, from the 19th-century Impressionists to modern-art students and sidewalk sketch vendors.*

⋏ *Chenonceaux Castle on the Cher River, in the center of France south of Paris, is one of the most beautiful of the many castles and châteaus in this part of the country.*

leadership, and morale; second, the French were politically divided and discouraged by a succession of unstable governments.

Marshal Philippe Pétain, who was now the French premier, requested a truce with the enemy. This truce brought France almost completely under German control and divided it into two parts. The larger part, which included all of northern and western France, was occupied by the Axis. The smaller part, southern France, was allowed its own government, but with restrictions that made it virtually dependent upon the enemy. Pétain now headed France's Vichy government, which collaborated with the Nazis of Germany. The Third Republic was ended.

Many patriotic Frenchmen refused to accept defeat. Most had fled to Britain, which welcomed all Allies who were determined to continue fighting the Axis forces. On June 18, 1940, one of them—General Charles de Gaulle, former French under secretary of war—launched a moving appeal to the French to resist the enemy. This triggered the formation of the Free French, whose ranks were considerably swelled during the war by civilians who had fled France.

Frenchmen who chose to remain at home and fight in secret were also inspired by de Gaulle. These secret fighters, called the Resistance, or French underground, performed heroic acts of sabotage, intelligence work, and widespread rebellion aimed at liberation.

On August 25, 1944, Paris was liberated. With the Allied forces racing across France to end the war, French nationalists rose to drive out the Nazis. The formal German surrender, marking the war's end in Europe, took place on May 8, 1945. The Axis forces were defeated.

# Fourth Republic

The French, like most Europeans, faced numerous difficulties and anxieties when the war ended. Their swift defeat in 1940 and the four-year occupation by Germany left the French with a deep sense

*American infantrymen march down the broad main boulevard of the Champs-Élysées in 1944, after freeing Paris from the Germans.*

of humiliation. General de Gaulle immediately set up a provisional government, which faced the daunting task of rebuilding the ruined country.

The Fourth Republic came into existence in 1946 with a constitution that was unacceptable to de Gaulle, who resigned in disgust even before the document went before the people for acceptance or rejection. De Gaulle felt that the constitution did not give enough authority to the head of the government, called the premier. Later developments suggested that the general was right. France's chief problem after the war was political rather than economic. Some 15 political parties were represented in the National Assembly; none was able to command a majority. To hold office, a premier had to depend on a coalition, formed by the support of several parties. This proved to be so difficult that France had 25 premiers between the end of World War II and the end of the Fourth Republic in 1958.

Despite political instability, the French economy made a rapid comeback. With financial aid from the United States, France was rebuilt. The economy recovered under the direction of Finance Minister Jean Monnet. Scientific research teams came together to develop atomic energy. Banks, coal mines, and gas and electricity companies were nationalized (made the property of the government). Industrial production—including chemical and electronic—expanded; the navy was revamped; and exports grew. In 1949 the United States proposed a military alliance of democratic countries in the North Atlantic region. France eagerly joined the other 11 founders of the North Atlantic Treaty Organization (NATO) in April 1949.

During the Fourth Republic, France's overseas holdings became troublesome. An eight-year war in Indochina (1946–54) cost lives and money. The people of this territory, which consisted of present-day Laos, Cambodia, and Vietnam, wanted independence, and France eventually granted it. Algeria, however, remained an extremely disturbing issue. In 1954 rebellion against French colonial rule broke out, and by 1958 the crisis threatened to topple the French government. France maintained an army of half a million men to keep control of Algeria, but some of the French people opposed the violent tactics that were used.

# Fifth Republic

In 1958 Charles de Gaulle was asked to return to political life, draw up a constitution, and lead the country. De Gaulle's constitution strengthened the powers of the president, who was elected for seven years. In December he was elected first president of the Fifth Republic. Many French feared that de Gaulle would become a dictator, but he remained true to the traditions of French democracy.

Under de Gaulle the Fifth Republic achieved a prosperity never equaled in French history. Much of this can be credited to American aid and the nationalization of some industries. Private enterprise was encouraged to expand under the guidance of a stable political regime. De Gaulle's France also enacted far-reaching social welfare measures. To reinforce France's claim as a world power, de Gaulle continued and expanded the Fourth Republic's atomic energy program, successfully testing the country's first atomic bomb in the Sahara Desert in 1960. In 1962 the French government negotiated a cease-fire with the Algerian rebels. Despite renegades in the French army who organized a secret terrorist campaign against Algerian freedom fighters, the North African colony achieved independence later that year. To achieve his goal of keeping France's military independent, the president withdrew all French forces from NATO in 1967.

In December 1965, Charles de Gaulle, at the age of 75, was reelected to a second term as president. His biggest challenge to maintaining his leadership became known as the Events of May 1968, when university students rebelled. The protest began as a call for educational reform, but it ultimately resulted in the fall of de Gaulle.

Industrial workers went on strike, joining the student protesters. The workers wanted more participation in management. By May 20, 7 million workers had laid down their tools; public services came to a halt; and transportation broke down. The protest and strikes caught de Gaulle unawares. He bounced back temporarily, though, by giving the nation an alternative: de Gaulle or chaos. De Gaulle's charisma triumphed, and the strikes ended. But his prestige had seriously diminished.

To reassure himself that France needed his leadership, the aging president proposed some constitutional reforms to the Senate. In 1969 he demanded that the voters respond to his proposals, which would have increased presidential power, and to his leadership. The opposition groups managed to turn the majority of the people against

*The charismatic leader of the Free French during World War II, Charles de Gaulle became the French premier in 1958, after drawing up a new constitution and establishing the Fifth Republic.*

*Student riots in Paris in May 1968 escalated and spread, bringing chaos to the streets and eventually bringing down de Gaulle's government.*

de Gaulle. When the vote was taken, the president's reforms were rejected. De Gaulle immediately resigned. He died the following year.

Presidential elections in June 1969 made Georges Pompidou the next president of France. Pompidou's term was no period of dramatic social or economic change. He continued the course toward economic power set by de Gaulle. With two years still to go as president, Pompidou died unexpectedly in April 1974.

Valéry Giscard d'Estaing, of the Independent Republicans party, was the next president. Giscard promised to make the country an "advanced liberal society." His reforms legalized abortion, made divorce easier to obtain, and reduced the voting age to 18. During his presidency, Giscard had to deal with the effects of the oil crisis, a worldwide recession brought on by increased oil prices. In France, as in most other countries, the recession brought ever-increasing inflation and unemployment.

Toward the end of the 1970s, the French Socialist party gained popularity. The 1981 presidential election made the Socialist François Mitterrand president. During Mitterrand's first few years in office, the government considered the nationalization of industry its highest priority. Under Mitterrand, France spent an estimated U.S. $10 billion of tax revenue to acquire banks and financial companies, steel and electronics concerns, and transportation and broadcasting networks. The Socialists insisted that nationalization would stimulate investment; private industry, however, went on an investment strike, resulting in a falling franc and the flight of capital abroad.

Mitterrand's government was further shaken by other developments. In 1985 an antinuclear protest ship owned by the environmentalist group Greenpeace was preparing to oppose French nuclear weapons testing in the South Pacific. Suddenly the ship was sunk at its dock in New Zealand. Though the French government at first denied any involvement, investigations soon proved that France's secret service had ordered the sinking. The ensuing scandal weakened the government.

By this time, France's attitude toward its minority populations, especially Arabs, was becoming an issue. There were allegations of Muslim involvement in terrorist attacks on French cities. Assaults on immigrants increased, and Jean-Marie Le Pen's ultraconservative National Front party emerged as a political force.

In the wake of these problems, the Socialist party lost its majority in the National Assembly in 1986, and Mitterrand was forced to accept "cohabitation" with a conservative parliament. Jacques Chirac, the new prime minister, began to reverse some Socialist programs by reprivatizing nationalized businesses and reducing regulatory controls and taxes. Although the Socialists regained the prime minister's post in 1988, the privatization policies continued in the 1990s.

By the early 1990s, the European Union (EU) emerged as a dominant issue in French politics. With the ratification of the Maastricht Treaty in 1992, France joined other European countries in working toward a unified Europe. Like the other nations, France agreed to strict economic guidelines for its budget deficit and national debt. Because these guidelines often demand higher taxes and cuts in social-welfare spending, they have been unpopular among many French citizens.

Economic woes (especially high unemployment), skepticism about the EU, and disenchantment with immigrants' competition for French jobs helped bring about the downfall of the Socialist government. In the 1993 parliamentary elections, a conservative center-right coalition of parties won a resounding victory. The next year,

*Jacques Chirac, France's president, addresses the United Nations General Assembly in New York. France continues to play a major, though sometimes controversial, role on the world stage.*

when Mitterrand finished his second term as president, he was succeeded by Jacques Chirac of the center-right coalition.

In the closing months of Mitterrand's term, 2,500 French troops moved into Rwanda to protect refugees during that country's civil war. Soon after being elected, Chirac called for greater international action to stem the bloody ethnic fighting in Bosnia and Herzegovina, and France provided the majority of ground troops for the peace mission. Despite these positive steps on the world stage, France drew intense criticism for its renewed testing of nuclear weapons in late 1995.

Meanwhile, the government's efforts to rein in its budget deficits were met with strikes and protests, and the unemployment rate remained high. A wave of terrorist bombings again raised the public's fear of foreigners. In 1997 Chirac called an early parliamentary election to seek a mandate for his policies, but the results were disastrous for the conservatives. Even though Prime Minister Alain Juppe tried to appease voters by announcing his resignation, a Socialist-led coalition regained the majority in the National Assembly.

Today, many divisions and uncertainties continue in French politics and society. The public's attitude toward the European Union is often wary if not hostile. Yet the policies of recent years have put France in a strong position to participate in the ongoing progress toward European unity. If the new era of prosperity promised by the EU's proponents does indeed materialize, France should be among the greatest beneficiaries.

An old man fishes from the banks of the Rhine River, near Strasbourg, France.
Although French life has changed, timeless scenes such as this are still common.

# People and Culture

France has 58 million inhabitants, with an average population density of 276 per square mile (107 per square kilometer). The island of Corsica, which has been part of France since the 18th century, has a population of 253,000. The Republic's overseas territories and departments together contain over 2 million people. Foreign residents — mainly from Portugal, Algeria, Morocco, Italy, and Spain — make up over six percent of France's population.

Virtually everyone in France speaks French, the official language of the country. Along with Spanish, Italian, and Portuguese, French is a member of the family of Romance languages, all descended from the Latin language of the Romans. When the Romans first invaded, the inhabitants of France (then Gaul) spoke Celtic dialects. Slowly, Celtic words and habits of speech modified the Latin. With the coming of the Germanic tribes in the 5th century A.D., still further changes took place in the French language.

In the 9th century French had become the spoken language of most Gauls; Latin still remained the written language. By the 13th century literary and historical works were being written in French. At the end of the 16th century French was considered the language of all cultivated people, and it became the common European language. In 1714 it was declared the official and universal language of diplomacy, a role it retained until World War I, when English came to share this distinction.

The official language of all of France's overseas departments and territories, French is spoken throughout the world today. It is the main or second language in 23 countries in Africa, 6 in Asia and the South Pacific, and 5 in Europe. French is spoken in many Caribbean islands and is the official language of Haiti. English and French are the two official languages of Canada.

French continues to influence English, as evidenced by the growing number of words and expressions incorporated into the English language. Some examples are c'est la vie (that's life), raison d'être (reason for living), faux pas (mistake), joie de vivre (joy of life), gourmet (a person with a refined taste in food), and bon appétit (enjoy your meal—a literal translation is "good appetite").

# French Cuisine

The word *cuisine*, literally "kitchen" in French, has come to mean "a characteristic manner or style of preparing food." French cuisine, over the centuries, has been associated with well-prepared and elaborate gastronomic adventures. The skill of the French in the preparation of superb dishes may be attributed to their traditional love of good food. Historically, they have had the "good appetite."

The Gauls shocked their Roman conquerors with their hearty appetite. Their dishes, anything but refined, consisted mainly of boiled meats and vegetables. Their national dish was whole wild boar stuffed with garlic and roasted on a spit. In the 9th century Emperor Charlemagne was recognized as something of a gourmet; his court held frequent elaborate feasts of roasted meat and peacock pies.

In the 17th century, during the reign of Louis XIV, coffee was introduced into France, and the first cafés (*café* is a literal translation

*French bakeries are renowned for their delicious specialties, including baguettes, croissants, and elaborate pastries.*

of "coffee") were opened. One of the king's mistresses established a cooking school for young women. Those who graduated with distinction were awarded a blue ribbon, the Cordon Bleu. Today, those who graduate from the cooking school of that name wear the same color ribbon, which has since distinguished the wearer as an excellent chef.

French culinary creations that have swept the world include the omelet, soufflés, quiche, pâté, mousse, croissants, crepes, French bread (baguette), french fries, and french toast. Two methods of French cooking have also gained worldwide usage: puree—to liquidize food by forcing it through a strainer; and sauté—to fry lightly in a shallow open pan.

Nowadays, a typical French meal involves a combination of the best food and wine. Breakfast and dinner are usually small; lunch is the main meal of the day. The daily menu of an average French family consists of the following: a *petit déjeuner* (breakfast) of café au lait (coffee with hot milk) for adults, hot chocolate for children, and tartines du beurre (slices of bread with butter) or croissants; a *déjeuner* (lunch) of appetizers followed by meat or fish and vegetables, a green salad with dressing, a dessert of pastry or fruit, wine, and café noir (black coffee); and a *dîner* (dinner) of soup, a light main course and vegetables, salad, cheese, dessert, and wine.

# Art, Literature, Fashion

As in its cuisine, France has excelled throughout the ages in the fine arts. The skill and brilliance of French artists has been expressed in numerous forms and styles. One of the highlights of French architecture was the development of the Gothic cathedral from the 12th to 16th centuries. These soaring, spacious marvels, particularly the cathedrals of Chartres, Reims, and Amiens and of Notre Dame in Paris, were profusely decorated with statues and impressive windows of bright stained glass that illustrated stories from the Bible.

In the 19th century painting was the preeminent French art form and was more highly regarded than that of Italy and Germany. In the 1870s a loose association of French artists introduced the style called Impressionism—opening up their canvases to the play of color, sunlight, and shadows and trying to paint things as they saw them, not as dictated by formal rules of art academies. Some of the well-known French Impressionists were Édouard Manet, Auguste Renoir, and Claude Monet. Paul Cézanne, Paul Gauguin, and Henri Matisse developed new styles that influenced much of the painting of the 20th century.

In the 20th century, French art has produced numerous isms, notably *cubism*, which is an attempt to portray the geometric elements of nature; *dadaism*, which uses ridicule and nonsense to reflect the meaninglessness of the modern world, and *surrealism*, which transforms traditional perceptions through unconscious, subconscious, and irrational elements.

The government has long subsidized the performing arts in France. Nine of the 54 theaters in Paris, including ballet and opera houses, are supported by the city or national government. To encourage theater in the rest of France, the government also subsidizes many other drama groups. In addition, the larger cities have municipal opera houses.

*Paul Cézanne (1839–1906) strongly influenced the development of 20th-century painting, especially the cubist movement. Many of his works depict the countryside in the south of France, where he lived and worked for several years.*

BALZAC A LA CANNE PAR

*Honoré de Balzac was one of France's greatest novelists. He wrote numerous novels; two of the most well known are* Le Père Goriot *and* Eugénie Grandet. *This sketch of him is by his friend, the noted caricaturist Honoré Daumier.*

Contemporary French music is distinguished by innovation and experimentation. Twentieth-century composers such as Claude Debussy and Maurice Ravel have become part of the great European musical tradition.

French literature has had a long and brilliant career. In the 9th century the *chansons de geste,* or songs of deed, centering around the exploits of Charlemagne, were the first literature in French. The 16th century produced a number of French literary figures, such as Rabelais, "the jester of France," and Montaigne, the brilliant essayist. During Louis XIV's reign Molière, Corneille, and Racine were the outstanding playwrights. Another prominent Frenchman in the 17th century was the philosopher René Descartes (1596–1650), who has been recognized as the father of modern philosophy. In the 18th century Voltaire and Rousseau captured the mind and soul of revolutionary France.

Victor Hugo and Honoré de Balzac were the chief writers of the early 19th century. Balzac, famous for his character portrayals, is ranked among the greatest of French novelists. Other prominent and influential French writers in the 19th century were Guy de Maupassant, Georges Sand, and Marcel Proust.

In the 20th century French philosophical writers came to the fore. Albert Camus (1913–60) and Jean-Paul Sartre (1905–80) explored the philosophy of existentialism. This mode of thought, which centers on the isolation of the individual in an indifferent society, greatly influenced the French and had an impact on world thinking.

The French are known for style, elegance, and sophistication. One who is well versed in the "good life" is said to have savoir faire. French words such as élan, panache, chic, and vogue—all of which are used in English—denote some manner of elegance or style. A connoisseur is a person who is especially knowledgeable in the arts or in matters of taste. That the French are connoisseurs of fashion, among other things, is undeniable. Some of the most highly regarded names in the field of fashion are French.

Most of these still maintain their base in Paris. Among them are Louis Vuitton; Yves Saint Laurent, considered the world leader in uncluttered, elegant clothes; and Christian Dior, which manufactures a clothing line as well as accessories. Pierre Cardin, who started his empire in the 1950s, covered all aspects of design, from fashion and furniture to sunglasses and cosmetics. His dress collections were varied and unpredictable.

Also based in Paris is the house of Chanel, producer of distinctive suits, bags, perfumes, and jewelry. Chanel No. 5 is perhaps the world's most famous perfume. Cartier, "the jeweler of kings and king of jewelers," has reigned in France's capital since 1898.

## Religion

In numbers, France is overwhelmingly a Catholic nation. Catholics account for 81 percent of the population; Muslims number about 4 million; Protestants, about 1 million; and Jews, about 750,000. A clear distinction must be made between practicing and nonpracticing Catholics. Although all Catholics are baptized, married, and buried by the church, only about 20 percent actually observe religious tenets — such as going to church.

Over the centuries the church's favors have seesawed. Before the Revolution the clergy belonged to the aristocratic class, taxing

*Many of France's world-famous perfumes are made from flowers from Grasse, a small town on the French Riviera. Approximately 100 pounds of flower petals are used to produce one-half pound of perfume essence.*

*The shrine of Lourdes in southwest France is revered by Catholics who believe that Bernadette Subirous saw a vision of the Virgin Mary there in 1858. The women shown here kneel before candles marking the spot in the grotto where Bernadette reported seeing the vision.*

and oppressing the peasants, as did the privileged nobles and the king. Napoléon reined in the clergy with the Concordat in 1801, a document that took away the church's claim to property and privileges in return for payments from the state. With the official separation of church and state in 1905 the church was again free to administer to the faithful.

Protestants have walked a rocky road in France. Their persecution by the Catholics culminated in the Wars of Religion in the 16th century. The 1598 Edict of Nantes protected the Protestants until Louis XIV revoked it in 1685. Protestants, today representing less than two percent of France's population, have continued to thrive. In May 1988 Michel Rocard was appointed prime minister of France, the fifth Protestant to attain that office.

Although religious tolerance is basic to the French, intolerance does appear from time to time, as in the Dreyfus affair of the late 1800s. Not until the 1990s did the nation acknowledge its role in the deportation of Jews to Nazi concentration camps during World War II. Recent years have witnessed renewed violence, inflammatory rhetoric, and ill-disguised legislation targeted against Jewish and Muslim minorities.

# Social Classes

Before the French Revolution, there were basically two classes in France—the privileged class, consisting of the nobles and the clergy, and the commoners, consisting of everyone else. After the Revolution, class lines became blurred. While the privileged class lost economic and traditional power and the masses gained vocal but not economic power, one ill-defined group, the bourgeoisie, arose.

The bourgeoisie, at that time, might be considered "middle class" because they were mainly traders and small businessmen. Over the coming centuries this group continued its upward mobility so that today the bourgeoisie is the dominant class in France. In the modern world, the dominant class is the one that possesses or effectively controls the major means of production.

In France today there are basically three broad social classes— the bourgeoisie, the petty bourgeoisie, and the working class. The bourgeoisie includes the industrialists, owners of big business, and decision-making technologists and bureaucrats. This class represents about 15 percent of the work force and controls the movement of money and resources. The petty bourgeoisie includes people who own or run medium-sized and small businesses, intellectuals, artists, teachers, supervisory personnel, and office workers. This class accounts for about 40 percent of the work force.

The third class, the working class, totals about 45 percent of the work force. It includes all those directly engaged in the production of material goods. The working class is occupied essentially in agriculture, industry, transport, public works, and construction. Its work is largely manual, or blue collar. The working class includes skilled and unskilled laborers and some service personnel.

## Living Standard

French values, habits, and life-styles have changed in the second half of the 20th century. The French now spend less on food and more on health, housing, travel, vacations, and education. They have also become easier spenders; installment buying is now common. Household appliances have become necessities rather than luxuries. Nighty-eight percent of French households own a refrigerator; 95 percent own a television set; 88 percent own a washing machine; and 77 percent own a car.

Urbanites have developed a passionate urge for a second residence—a house in the country to which they can escape on weekends. For the French, living the good life seems to have replaced politics as the favorite leisure-time preoccupation. A more luxurious life is now easily accessible to most of the French because increases in the country's economic production since 1950 have produced, among other things, the highest living standard in France's history.

Another factor contributing to increased spending power is the low birthrate of the French. Throughout recent decades the number of births has hovered around two per family. With a small family it is easier to take advantage of the good life.

Sporting activities are an integral part of leisure time. The most popular team sport is soccer. There are almost 8,000 organized soccer clubs in France. Other popular pastimes are bicycling, skiing, mountain climbing, tennis, and swimming.

The women of the Republic have fared well in contemporary times. Granted the right to vote in 1945 and guaranteed absolute equality of rights by the constitution, French women have been

*The Tour de France, which lasts three weeks and covers over 2,400 miles (3,900 kilometers), is considered the most prestigious bicycle race in the world. Each year, thousands of people watch the racers along the grueling course.*

elected to the parliament, and in 1991 Edith Cresson became the nation's first female prime minister. Women make up 45 percent of the work force. Though many of the jobs held by women in France are in the garment and textile industries and in retail trade, the proportion of women in the professions and in executive and managerial positions is growing.

# Celebrations

Many holidays are celebrated throughout the year—some religious, some historical, some national. To celebrate the New Year, festivities are held on the evening of December 31 and through the night with an elaborate supper. At midnight family and friends kiss under the mistletoe. To commemorate the Epiphany (Feast of the Kings, January 6), a large round pastry containing a hidden bean is baked, portions are distributed at random, and the person who finds the bean becomes the king or queen for the evening. Mardi Gras, the day before the start of Lent, the 40-day period of preparation for Easter, is celebrated in February. The Mardi Gras celebration features parades of giant cardboard figures and flowered floats.

May 1, Labor Day, became a French legal holiday in 1947; it is celebrated with workers' parades. May 8 is also a legal holiday, marking the end of World War II. France's National Day is July 14. It commemorates the storming of the Bastille, the start of the French Revolution in 1789. In celebration, parades are held during the day, followed by fireworks and dancing in the street at night. On Christmas Eve, the French go to midnight mass. Local customs are numerous and include torchlight processions on skis in the Alps.

# Education

With a literacy rate of 99 percent (this means that 99 percent of adults can read and write), France is one of the most literate countries in the world. Education in the French republic is compulsory from ages 6 to 16. Public education is free, including all textbooks through the second year of secondary school. Private schools may also have their textbooks supplied free of charge. The ministry of education establishes a uniform curriculum for the entire country.

Most private schools follow the state system of education to prepare their students for the regular government-sanctioned diplomas. About 15 percent of French students attend private school at the preschool and elementary levels, and approximately 23 percent attend private secondary school.

French children attend school Monday, Tuesday, Thursday, Friday, and half a day on Saturday. Classes run from 8:30 A.M. to noon and continue after lunch from 2:00 P.M. to 5:00 P.M. On Wednesday, French television has programs specifically geared to children.

Preschool education, though optional, has become increasingly popular with parents. Preschool activities are not academic but rather social and creative. Children attend elementary school from ages 6 to 11. First they are taught the basic elements of learning—reading, writing, and arithmetic. These three subjects take up most of the 29 hours they spend in school each week; the rest of the time is divided between academic activities (history, geography, civics, music, and art) and physical education.

Secondary education, which follows elementary schooling, is pursued at two levels. Attendance is required through *collège*, the first level, which corresponds to junior high school in the United States. In collège, students continue their studies in foreign languages, economics, natural and applied science, and vocational and technical training. Upon the successful completion of collège studies, which usually requires four years, the student receives a diploma, the *brevet des collèges*.

Those who wish to continue their studies—and can pass the qualifying exams—advance to *lycée*, the second level of secondary school. About 25 percent of collège graduates usually move on to lycée. Here, students may select one of two tracks. The first program lasts two years and is essentially technical and vocational. The second program, an academic one, covers three years, preparing students for the *baccalauréat* exam, a prerequisite for admission to university.

In France the number of students who continue from collège to lycée and then on to university is comparatively small because French students receive early vocational and technical training to prepare them for their chosen careers.

# Health and Welfare

The social security system benefits the French throughout their life, providing them with health insurance, family allowances, old-age pension, and welfare. For health, maternity, disability, old-age, and life insurance the employer pays two-thirds of the contribution, and the employee pays one-third. The employer pays the total amount for occupational accidents and family allowances.

Health insurance covers medical expenses, dental bills, maternity costs, disability payments, and death benefits. All households

*One of the numerous local religious celebrations is the annual blessing of the boats at fishing villages by the sea.*

with two or more dependent children are eligible to receive the family allowance, regardless of marital or occupational status. Family allowance benefits are also paid to the legal guardians of orphaned children, single parents, and parents with handicapped children.

Good health for a child begins even before it is born. Prenatal allowances are paid after the expectant mother completes three free prenatal medical exams. Babies also receive three free medical check-ups during their first two years of life. As a result of such care, France's infant mortality rate (the number of infants who die before their first birthday) is quite low — less than 6 per 1,000 live births.

Because of the great care taken by the state, France's population is a healthy one. The average man lives to the age of 74, the

*The excellent education system in France has made it one of the most literate countries in the world. These children attend a school in Paris.*

average woman to about 82. The chief causes of death are circulatory diseases (33 percent) and cancer (27 percent).

People who request welfare must show that they are unable to provide for their own needs. Welfare payments are made only to permanent residents on French territory. Among those eligible for welfare benefits are vagrants, ex-prisoners, and former mental patients who lack the income necessary for everyday life.

*May 1989 marked the 100-year anniversary of the Eiffel Tower, an instantly recognizable Parisian landmark, erected to commemorate the centennial of the French Revolution. Sound-and-light shows, fireworks, and special lighting marked the celebration of the tower's anniversary and the bicentennial of the French Revolution.*

# The Urbanization of France

After World War II, when the government greatly emphasized industrialization in France, the small farmer who could not cope with mechanization left the land. In 1948 the proportion of farmers in the work force was 35 percent; by 1988 it had fallen to 8 percent, and by the late 1990s to 4 percent. Farming required larger investments, and only the bigger and more efficient units survived.

The decrease in the number of farmers was not due only to the cost of mechanization. Factories sprang up in urban areas. The lure of city lights, the excitement of a bustling metropolis, and the escape from a rough farming existence drew many countryfolk to the world of concrete and steel.

Despite the movement away from the land — today 74 percent of the population live in urban areas — French agricultural production has continued to outstrip the rest of Western Europe. Mechanization and modern farming methods have contributed to the supremacy of French agriculture. Today, 55 percent of the land surface is used for farming.

There is, however, another facet to rural life in France. *La terre*, the land, holds an almost mystical association for the French. Many

French have a romantic vision of the countryman as the symbol of hard work, individual enterprise, frugality, and common sense—a reflection of what many see as the qualities of the nation as a whole. This mythology of rural life has become an important part of French culture. Thus, while the drift of people from the country to the cities goes on, nostalgia for the land endures. It is reflected in the growing number of city dwellers who are snapping up abandoned farmhouses and building new ones as weekend and vacation retreats.

## Paris

Throughout France's history, all major aspects of French life—culture, politics, administration, and business—have had their source in Paris, the capital. Paris is the home of style, fashion, and sidewalk cafés, yet its streets have often been the battleground of political and economic ideas. Metropolitan Paris, with a population of 10.7 million (the city proper has 2.2 million), is located in the northern part of the country.

The streets of Paris have no definite plan, for the city was old long before people thought of building streets wide and straight. Numerous bridges span the Seine River, which winds its way through the center of Paris. The city abounds in beautiful parks and squares, museums and theaters, churches and cathedrals.

France's capital continues to be the source of the largest number of jobs in such fields as government, law, higher education, and the service industries. Paris is also the country's main center of business activity, and virtually all of France's big banks, insurance companies, and manufacturing firms have their headquarters here.

Like all major cities, Paris contains several districts, or *quartiers*, that differ in appearance and in subtle characteristics of the inhabitants. One such quartier is Île Saint-Louis, a village located in the Seine in the middle of Paris, connected by six bridges to the mainland. On Île Saint-Louis the launderer uses a flatiron instead of an electric iron, the baker bakes bread in a wood-burning oven, and the glazier walks about with huge panes of glass strapped to his back, calling out, *"Vitrier!"* (French for glazier, one who sets glass). On this island you can have your scissors sharpened, your chimney swept, and your chairs recaned, all by itinerant tradespeople. Île Saint-Louis remains a perfectly preserved bit of the 17th century, almost untouched by modernization.

West of Île Saint-Louis, on the southern bank of the Seine, is the VIIᵉ (7th) Arrondissement (district). Here reside politicians, dip-

*In the heart of Paris, the Île de la Cité and Île Saint-Louis sit in the middle of the Seine River. Both islands are connected to the mainland by bridges but are far removed in atmosphere from the rest of busy, modern Paris.*

*The focus of the Musée d'Orsay, built in a renovated railway station to house 19th-century French art, is the enormous central hall, lined with sculptures.*

lomats, journalists, and what remains of the French nobility. The Soviet, Italian, Australian, Dutch, and Swiss ambassadors all have splendid town houses in the VII$^e$. Also located in this district are ministry offices, the prime minister's official residence, and the French Parliament.

The VII$^e$ is the most protected part of Paris. With low crime rates, clean streets, and 17th-, 18th-, and 19th-century private residences, it is a kind of open architectural museum. Some of Paris's finest shops and restaurants are located in this quartier. On the opposite bank of the Seine is the VIII$^e$ (8th) Arrondissement district, where Paris's—and the world's—foremost fashion houses and jewelers base their establishments.

Montmartre is another village within the city. Located in the north of Paris, Montmartre has resisted all efforts at modernization. This may explain its attraction for the omnipresent tourists, who can be found here at any time of the day or night. Charming and quiet, Montmartre is famous for its wine bars, cabarets, and theater cafés; it even produces its own wine.

The fastest-growing district in Paris today is Le Marais, on the east bank of the Seine. The construction of the Bastille Opera has turned this previously stagnating area into a scene of cultural revival. Conceived by France's president as the "people's opera house," the Bastille Opera stands on the site of the old prison. It was dedicated on July 14, 1989, the 200th anniversary of the storming of the Bastille that marked the beginning of the French Revolution. It has the largest auditorium in France (seating 2,700), a basement amphitheater for concerts, a studio theater for smaller performances, a library, and rehearsal rooms.

The Left Bank—the bohemian district of Paris, situated on the left bank of the Seine—is the capital's equivalent of New York City's Greenwich Village. Saint-Germain and Montparnasse are two regions on the Left Bank where writers, artists, and musicians live. On weekdays and weekends alike, the Boulevard du Montparnasse and small neighboring streets attract crowds of people to their cafés, cinemas, and restaurants.

Two of Paris's newest entertainment and educational centers are La Villette and the Musée d'Orsay. Located in the northeast corner of Paris, La Villette brings together a rich combination of elements: parks, meadows, fountains, recreation, the arts, science, and technology. The Musée d'Orsay, in the heart of Paris, opened its doors in 1987. Adapted from an old railway station and a hotel, this museum specializes in exhibits of art from 1848 to 1914.

Of all the structures adorning the city, four stand out as symbols of Paris and France: the Arc de Triomphe, the Eiffel Tower, the Louvre, and Notre Dame. Located in the west of the capital, the Arc de Triomphe was built (1806–36) to commemorate the victories of Napoléon Bonaparte. In the VII$^e$ Arrondissement is the Eiffel Tower, a masterpiece of metal construction. It was erected in 1889 to mark the centennial of the French Revolution.

Statues, paintings, and relics are among the forms of priceless art contained in the Louvre, considered the greatest art museum in the world. Located on the east bank of the Seine, the Louvre consists of several structures. The oldest, begun in 1204, was once a fortress and a prison; the building known as the Old Louvre was completed in the mid-1600s; the New Louvre was completed 300 years later.

*Millions of visitors flock to the Louvre to view its incomparable collection of paintings, sculptures, and decorative arts. Its most famous treasures include Leonardo da Vinci's Mona Lisa and the ancient sculptures the Victory of Samothrace and the Venus de Milo.*

Recent additions have increased the museum's exhibition space to more than 750,000 square feet (70,000 square meters).

On Île de la Cité in the Seine River is Notre Dame cathedral. This stately Catholic church, a prime tourist attraction, is an outstanding example of Gothic architecture. Unusual features are the two square towers on the west front and the massive flying buttresses (stone props) that support the roof. The building was begun in 1163 but was not completed until early in the 14th century.

As with many of the smaller French cities, Paris is surrounded by a ring of industrial suburbs. Large plants that manufacture electrical goods, chemicals, machinery, automobiles, and aircraft are generally located in the inner suburbs, especially to the north and to the south of the city. Paris's outer suburbs are expanding rapidly as a large number of young couples and their children are settling in these areas.

## Other Cities

Paris is undeniably the center of French life. But some of France's other cities, although not as well known, are worthy of attention. Among them is Versailles, situated 12 miles southwest of Paris. The town's most noted building is the Palace of Versailles. Now a tourist attraction, the palace is a treasure house of relics dating back to the time of Clovis. Terraced gardens, pools, beautiful fountains, and decorative trees and shrubbery surround the imposing palace structure. Versailles and its magnificent palace remain a beautiful illustration of the French monarchy's splendor.

To the northeast of Paris is the city of Lille, a large, densely populated industrial area. With its coal-mining and textile-manufacturing suburbs, Lille — with a population of 1 million — is France's fourth largest city. Marseilles, located in the southeast, on the Mediterranean coast, is the country's principal seaport and a diversified manufacturing center. It is also the Republic's third largest city, with a population of 1.2 million inhabitants. Marseilles is credited with giving France its national anthem, the "Marseillaise," which was sung by Marseilles soldiers entering Paris in 1792 during the French Revolution. Farther east, along the coast of the Mediterranean, are the resort cities of Cannes, site of one of the largest annual international film festivals, and Nice, a mecca for European vacationers.

France's second largest city is Lyons, with a population of 1.3 million. A commercial and industrial metropolis, Lyons is situated in east-central France. Because it is located at the point where the Rhône and Saône rivers flow together, it had become a center of trade by the 5th century. Beginning in the 15th century, Lyons became famous for producing beautiful silk fabrics.

The city of Bordeaux lies in southwest France, at the center of one of the most famous wine-producing regions in the world. Once the capital of the ancient Roman province of Aquitania and the center

*The city of Bordeaux is surrounded by thriving vineyards. The grapes grown here are used to make the well-known wine to which the region gives its name.*

*At high tide the small island of Mont-Saint-Michel is completely surrounded by water, providing a dramatic setting for its ancient Benedictine abbey.*

of the fiercely independent former region of Gascony, Bordeaux now has a population of 700,000. Held by the English from 1152 to 1453, the city retains an English flavor. By the 14th century the English had firmly established a thriving export market for the red wine of the region, which they call claret. Their influence lives on; many long-established merchant families give their sons such English names as Nathaniel, Archibald, and Edward.

Throughout the French republic the old cohabits successfully with the new. Medieval towns such as Crécy-la-Chapelle, Moret-sur-Loing, and Provins are found in eastern France. In the Gulf of St.-Malo, in northwestern France, the church of Mont-Saint-Michel rests on a rocky isle, site of a 6th-century Benedictine abbey. Renaissance castles are located all over the country; the most renowned are at Fontainebleu and in the Loire Valley.

*The French economy is healthy, but the past 20 years have been marked by numerous strikes called by workers demanding better salaries and improved labor conditions.*

# Government

France is governed under the 1958 constitution that brought about the Fifth Republic. This constitution, drafted by Charles de Gaulle, provides the president with a stronger role in government than he had previously held. According to the constitution, governmental power is shared among the president, the prime minister and his cabinet, and Parliament, which consists of the National Assembly and the Senate.

The president appoints the prime minister, who recommends to the president the 26 ministers of the cabinet. Among his other constitutional powers, the president proposes legislation; signs all laws into effect; presides at cabinet meetings; and may dissolve the National Assembly if he desires a new one. In short, under the French system of government, although the president is "head of state" and the prime minister is "head of government," the president is free either to impose his will on matters of government or to allow the prime minister, the cabinet, and Parliament to determine policy.

The president of the Republic of France is elected directly by the people for a term of 7 years; French citizens who are at least 18 years old are eligible to vote. The French vote according to a two-round majority system. If no presidential candidate gets a clear majority of votes in the first round, the electors vote a second time the following week for one of the top two vote getters from the first round.

Election of the 577-member National Assembly is similar. If no party obtains a majority of representatives in the first round, the voters return to the polls one week later. An electoral college elects the 321 senators for a term of 9 years; one-third of the Senate is renewed every 3 years.

The president, the prime minister, and the cabinet compose the executive branch of government; the National Assembly and the Senate make up the legislative branch. Bills pass through both legislative chambers. In the event of disagreement, a joint committee is set up to produce a compromise piece of legislation. Parliament—these two chambers—sits for two regular sessions, each lasting three months, one beginning in April and the other in October.

For administrative purposes, France is divided into 96 departments, which are similar to states in the United States. Departments are divided into smaller units, like U.S. counties, that are called *arrondissements*. These in turn are subdivided into *communes*, or townships. A general council, headed by its president, administers the affairs of each department. A representative of the national government, named by the cabinet, sits on the general council of each department.

A municipal council, elected by the people, governs each commune. A mayor is elected from among the council members. The mayor develops laws and regulations and puts them into practice, drafts and submits the budget for the commune, and has authority over the municipal police to maintain security and public order. Another important function of the mayor is performing marriages. All marriages in France must be performed by a mayor or his deputy before any religious ceremony can take place.

*Floodlights illuminate the National Assembly building in a celebration of Paris's founding on July 8.*

France's judicial system is administered by a number of different courts. Civil courts rule on disputes between private parties. Criminal courts—of which there are several, differentiated according to the severity of the crime—deal with violations of the law. Judgments at this level may be appealed to higher courts, of which there are different types for different offenses. The Republic's highest appellate court is the Court of Cassation. Special courts, called administrative tribunals, handle disagreements between private parties and the various government services. The death penalty was abolished in France in 1981.

French men are required to register for military service at the age of 18. They may put off active service until the age of 22 if some personal situation warrants it, such as pursuit of education, poor health, or a dependent family. Active service usually lasts 12 months. Conscientious objectors, those who refuse to bear arms or participate in military service because of religious or moral principles, are required to perform some work of public service for at least 24 months.

The French have traditionally aligned themselves in one of two camps—the Left or the Right. Many parties have entered and exited the political scene in France down the ages, but the concepts of Left and Right have existed since the time of the French Revolution, when the radicals sat on the left side of the assembly and the conservatives sat on the right.

Today, there are five significant parties on the French political scene—three large and two small. On the Left are the Socialist party

*President François Mitterrand inspects an honor guard on a visit to London in 1984. Elected on a Socialist platform in 1981, he made his policies more moderate upon his reelection in 1988.*

and the smaller Communist party. On the Right are the Rally for the Republic (RPR), the Union for French Democracy (UDF), and an ultraconservative party called the National Front.

The Socialist party stands for a planned economy, national independence, and promoting the interests of the workers through nationalization of industries. The Communist party wants to transform the capitalist society into a collectivist one in which property will be equally shared. To achieve this, it calls for a fraternal society of workers, intellectuals, and farmers.

The RPR is identified as a Gaullist party because it supports the political ideals of former president de Gaulle: national independence, a strong military, limited government intervention in the economy, and opposition to communism. The UDF, usually referred to as the Conservative party, promotes an economy free of state intervention and endorses the ideals of democracy. The National Front, or extreme right, calls for an end to immigration and the return of immigrants to their native lands.

Although France's political parties have traditionally affiliated themselves with either the Left or the Right, they always remain separate and distinct. They do, however, ally themselves when they find it useful. Especially in recent years, French politics has been marked by alliances between various parties.

## Economy and Resources

During the 1970s the French economy grew at an average rate of 3.5 percent, a pace that was faster than that of the rest of Europe and the United States. However, its annual growth rate decreased during the 1980s and 1990s to fall slightly behind those of Germany, Britain, and Italy and well behind that of the United States. Despite this economic slowdown, the French republic remains among the world's leaders in agriculture, industry, and technology.

France is the largest agricultural producer in Western Europe. The country's principal agricultural products are cereals (fifth in world production) and dairy products (fifth in world production of milk). Fruit and vegetables are grown in all regions of the country, particularly in the south. Ranked as the world's first or second largest producer of wine (depending on the yearly crop yield), France has extensive vineyards, especially in Burgundy and around Bordeaux. Forests cover about 27 percent of the country. Small iron ore deposits and coal are found in the northeast; natural gas is found in the southwest.

Industrial areas are scattered throughout the country, but the heaviest concentrations are in the Paris region and in the Rhône Valley in the southeast. These were the original industrial areas, based on mining, metalworking, and textiles. Today, the liveliest French industries are motor vehicles, pharmaceuticals, aerospace, wool, and textiles. France is the home of Airbus Industrie, Europe's largest aircraft maker.

Following Russia and the United States, France ranks third as a world nuclear power. The French government spends approximately 16 percent of the national budget in order to maintain the country's military.

France's military might is not only evident in its national defenses forces; the country also ranks high in the world of arms sales. The nation's chief customers for military goods are Middle Eastern oil-exporting countries, from which it obtains its energy supply. Oil is France's main import; the country depends on imports to satisfy more than 50 percent of its energy needs. France's main customers for its other exports—manufactured goods, chemicals, wine, and foodstuffs—are the European Union and the United States. A sizable proportion of France's resources goes to its overseas departments and territories. Significant amounts, too, are sent abroad as aid to underdeveloped countries, particularly in Africa.

*France's industries and technology contribute greatly to its economic base. This factory is located on the Rhine in northeastern France.*

The French unit of currency is the *franc*, divided into 100 *centimes*. Recently one U.S. dollar has been equivalent to roughly 6 francs. In the mid-1990s France's GDP (gross domestic product) was equivalent to approximately U.S. $1.5 trillion. A majority of the working population (69 percent) is engaged in the services sector; 27 percent work in industry; and 4 percent farm the land. The average yearly wage is approximately U.S. $26,000.

France's economy has appeared to be improving in recent years, though unevenly. The inflation rate, or rate at which money loses its buying power, decreased from 12 percent in the early 1980s to less than 2 percent by the late 1990s. The unemployment rate, nevertheless, continued to hover between 11 and 13 percent. For France to have a healthy, stable, and competitive economy, both inflation and unemployment need to be kept under control.

*On March 25, 1957, in Rome, French foreign minister Christian Pineau (third from left, seated at table) signed, along with representatives from five other European countries, the pact creating the European Economic Community.*

## The European Union

The European Union (EU) is an organization of European countries that attempts to integrate the economies, coordinate the foreign policies, and eventually perhaps bring about the political union of all the member states. Today's EU has evolved gradually, changing its name as its ambitions have increased. It was founded in 1958 as the European Economic Community, frequently known as the EEC or Common Market. France was one of the founding members, as were Belgium, West Germany, Italy, Luxembourg, and the Netherlands. In 1967 the organization became known as the European Union, or EC. Finally, by 1994, the current name and structure took shape.

From its beginning to the mid-1980s, the organization maintained some degree of economic cooperation; for example, tariffs (import duties) were abolished among the member countries. True unity, however, was lacking. In 1985, a former French minister of finance, Jacques Delors, became president of the European Commission, the group's executive body. He proposed a way to make the community a barrier-free, competitive market in which goods, services, people, and money could move freely from one region to another. National barriers would be abolished and common economic policies instituted. Only such a union, it was argued, could give European nations the economic and political clout to match countries like the United States, Russia, China, India, and Japan.

The capstone to these developments was the Maastricht Treaty, transforming the European Community into the European Union and calling for a single European currency (the *euro*) to be phased into use starting at the end of the century. France and the newly reunified Germany, nervous at the prospect that poorer members might drag down the economies of stronger members, demanded that strict guidelines be set for the national economies of all members wishing to participate in the single-currency plan. The most notable of these guidelines concerned budget deficits and national debts: a nation's annual budget deficit could not exceed 3 percent of its GDP, and its total national debt could not exceed 60 percent of its GDP. Even France and Germany have had difficulty meeting these criteria.

Within France, as in other European nations, the economic austerity demanded by the single-currency guidelines has provoked some resistance. Many French people are also suspicious of other EU goals, such as a common European defense, a common justice system, and common standards for immigration. The French people value their independence and their culture, and they worry that the EU's development may undermine the uniqueness they have cherished for centuries.

France's modernized railroads are an important link in its transportation system. This high-speed train, called the TGV, is one of the fastest in the world.

# Transportation and Communications

The extreme centralization of French life in Paris is reflected in the transportation network. The pattern was set by early rulers and reinforced by Napoléon, who built a system of major roads that came from all parts of the country to meet in the heart of the city. France has well-developed networks of railroads, highways, and waterways, but their excessive concentration in Paris often makes direct travel between provincial towns and industrial complexes difficult, especially in the south of France.

The railroads, which are very modern, are owned and operated by the state, which spends three times as much on the railroads as it does on the highways. With 21,173 miles (34,074 kilometers) of railway, France's railroad network is one of the largest in the world. Train service is fast, and traffic volume is large. In 1990 the Train á Grande Vitesse (high-speed train) between Paris and Lyons set a new speed record — 320.2 miles per hour (515 kilometers per hour). The TGV, as it is called, still runs the fastest regularly scheduled passenger trains in the world.

France's highway and road network — 504,055 miles, or 811,200 kilometers—carries a large volume of passengers and goods. The country has about 25 million automobiles. Trucks and commercial vehicles carry the majority of the domestic freight. Traffic is very heavy and increases about 10 percent every year.

More than 1 million city workers commute to central Paris each day. Most suburban commuters travel on surface railroads; others take buses to the nearest Métro (subway) terminal. The Métro is an efficient but crowded means of transportation. Besides the regular Métro, inaugurated in 1900, Paris now has an express Métro, which provides service to the suburbs and nearby towns. Marseilles, Lyons, and Lille also have subway service.

France has 9,278 miles (14,932 kilometers) of internal waterways, both rivers and canals. Less than 5 percent of domestic freight in France moves by water. Along the French coastline are a large number of sea harbors, which yearly handle hundreds of millions of tons of cargo coming into and leaving the country. Three of these—at Marseilles, Le Havre, and Dunkerque—were greatly enlarged in the 1970s and are among the largest international harbors. These three handle two-thirds of France's maritime trade.

The major share of both passenger and freight air traffic is carried by the national airlines, Air France and Air Inter. Additionally, there are a number of small airlines, some of them privately owned and some controlled by nationalized companies. Air France has one of the most extensive networks of air routes in the world. Paris has two international airports: Charles de Gaulle Airport in the northeast and Orly Airport in the south.

# Communications

There are about 50 million radios and 30 million television sets in France; all broadcasting is overseen by a government agency. Radio France, the national radio network, operates three national stations: France-Inter (news, music, and variety programs), France-Culture

*French publishers produce more than 30,000 books each year. Many of them are sold and resold in the numerous bookstalls that line the streets on the Left Bank of the Seine in Paris. This district is the site of the Sorbonne, a university that was founded in 1253.*

(lectures on art, literature, and music), and France-Musique (jazz and classical music). Radio France also operates 20 regional stations and 32 local stations in major cities across the country. Additionally, there are some 1,800 privately owned radio stations.

The government also operates Radio France International (RFI), which broadcasts international programs and produces shows designed for international distribution, including programs in foreign languages for various countries and in French for French citizens living abroad. With a total of 25 stations, RFI has an audience of 80 million. Radio France Outre-Mer (RFO) is responsible for producing and broadcasting radio and television programming for the French overseas departments and territories. Programs from nearby countries can be received in most parts of France.

In France, every household with a television set must pay an annual tax, or license, to the government, which distributes this revenue to the TV companies. The companies are financed not only through license fees but also through advertising and other earnings, such as program sales. There are six TV networks: two government owned and four privately owned.

The main state-owned television network is Antenne 2, or A2, established in 1972. Approximately 50 percent of A2 programming is devoted to entertainment, 47 percent to news, and 3 percent to advertising. A2 captures about 45 percent of the French TV-viewing audience. France's largest privately owned TV network is TF1, or Société Nationale de Télévision Française. TF1 began broadcasting France's first TV programs in 1937. Its programming is 50 percent entertainment, 46 percent news, and 4 percent advertising. Cable TV is now available as well.

France's 31 million telephone subscribers can use Minitel, a telecommunications system that combines the telephone and the computer. With Minitel, users can shop, pay bills, make reservations, play video games, get stock market reports, and chat with each other—all by computer. Launched in 1982, Minitel, the largest such system in the world, grew to 6 million units by the end of 1994.

France has 116 daily newspapers with a combined circulation of more than 11 million. Some of the most widely circulated are published in Paris: *Le Monde*, *Le Figaro*, *France-Soir*, and *Le Parisien Libéré*. Most French newspapers have clearly defined political positions. For example, *Le Monde* sides with the Left, and *Le Figaro* leans to the Right.

Some of France's popular magazines are *Paris-Match*, *L'Express*, and *Le Point*, (newsweeklies); *Elle* (women's weekly); and *Jours de France* and *Point de Vue* (social weeklies). Additionally, the country's 400 publishing houses produce some 30,000 new books every year.

*Inaugurated on the 200th anniversary of the French Revolution, the spectacular (and controversial) Grande Arche of the Place de la Défense in Paris suggests a futuristic vision of French culture.*

# Future Perspectives

Two centuries ago, a brutal revolution signaled the French people's hatred for the oppressive rule of their king; it announced their desire to govern themselves. Today, as a prosperous democratic country and a world power, France finds itself tempted to look back on its rich heritage at the same time that it must face novel, and sometimes unforeseen, challenges.

Perhaps France's greatest strength has been its distinctive and zealously nurtured national identity, the identity that found such a tumultuous expression in the Revolution. In the current world, however, many French people fear their specialness may be lost as more and more nations with their own agendas come under the umbrella of the European Union (EU). They worry that if everyone on the Continent is European, no one will be truly French. Nevertheless, the benefits of French cooperation with the EU are already manifesting themselves in rising tourism, greater business opportunities, and educational exchanges. Exactly how the French will weigh the benefits and liabilities of the EU in future years is hard to predict. After weathering the belt-tightening needed to prepare for a common currency, France still must decide how to reconcile its culture, its needs for defense and security, and its attitudes toward immigration and relief for refugees with those of its neighbors. Of course, the other EU countries are facing similar dilemmas.

At the same time, many of France's most difficult challenges can be found at home. The republic's persistently high rate of unemployment has stymied politicians of both the Left and the Right. In recent years, scandals have damaged almost all the traditional political parties, and the decline of public confidence in moderate politicians has led to successes by the extremist National Front in parliamentary and municipal elections.

France's overseas territories and former colonies have their own agendas, too. Though most residents of the territories appear content with the status quo, independence movements are active in all of France's possessions. New Caledonia experienced a wave of violence and protests in the 1980s. After France's resumption of nuclear testing in the Pacific Ocean in 1995, opponents of French Polynesia's territorial status attacked and burned the international airport at Papeete, Tahiti.

Former French colonies in Africa probably pose the greatest potential difficulties overseas. France's close relationship with most of them embroils France in their internal conflicts. Civil wars, like those in Rwanda and Burundi, will probably continue to arise sporadically, and French troops will be called upon to separate combatants and protect French citizens. More ominous is the reaction that has met Algerian immigrants in France: murderous attacks on Muslims, retaliatory terrorism against French interests, inflammatory rhetoric from the far Right, and increasing legislation to limit immigration. Reminders that nationalism has an ugly side are always close at hand.

Nevertheless, France will continue to have its simpler sources of pride. The soil will produce fine wines and abundant crops; the

*The past glories of France are carefully conserved for future generations. This historic château on the Loire River is one of many that dot the region.*

schools will graduate future leaders who may now have a wider arena for their accomplishments; the factories will ship cars and planes for foreign markets; new designers will change the look of the world as their predecessors have done. As the French say, *Le plus ça change, le plus c'est la même chose.* The more things change, the more they stay the same.

# ◄GLOSSARY►

**Ancien régime**  French for "old regime." The system that existed before the Revolution whereby the monarchy, the nobles, and the clergy held privileges and power that were denied commoners.

**Bourgeoisie**  The dominant class in France today. This class includes industrialists, people in big business, and decision-making technologists.

*Chansons de geste*  Translated as "songs of deed." These songs were the first forms of written literature in French. They centered around the exploits of Emperor Charlemagne in the 9th century.

*Collège*  The first level of secondary education, corresponding to junior high school in the United States. Study at this level usually lasts 4 years, from age 11 to age 15.

*Connoisseur*  A person especially knowledgeable in the arts or matters of taste.

*Cuisine*  *Kitchen* in French, the word now signifies a characteristic manner or style of preparing food.

**Gourmet**  A person with a refined taste in food.

**Guillotine**  A device used for execution by beheading.

**Huguenots**  The people of France who adopted the Protestant religion. In the 16th and 17th centuries they were persecuted by the Catholics.

**Limon**  Loess, a rich, fine-grained soil prevalent in France. It is especially productive in the cultivation of cereals and root crops.

**Lycée**  The second level of secondary school. One program is of two years' duration, consisting mainly of technical studies; the alternative program, lasting three years, prepares students for university.

**Quartiers**  Districts of French cities, especially Paris, that differ in characteristics of the inhabitants, appearance, and atmosphere.

**Resistance**  Name for the French underground during World War II. These secret fighters engaged in sabotage and intelligence work against the Nazi forces occupying France.

**Savoir faire**  Literally "to know to do," this now denotes one who is well versed in the "good life." One knowledgeable in the art of living is said to have savoir faire.

**Third Estate**  Before the Revolution, a social class that fell below the privileged classes of monarchy, nobles, and clergy in social standing.

# ◄ I N D E X ►

◄ 125 ►